Close
Encounters

Close
Encounters

JEWISH VIEWS ABOUT GOD

Ronald H. Isaacs

JASON ARONSON INC.
Northvale, New Jersey
London

This book was set in 12 pt. Garamond by Aerotype, Inc.

Library of Congress Cataloging-in-Publication Data

Isaacs, Ronald H.
    Close encounters : Jewish views about God / Ronald H. Isaacs.
      p. cm.
    Includes bibliographical references and index.
    ISBN 1-56821-915-6 (alk. paper)
    1. God (Judaism)—History of doctrines. I. Title.
    BM610.I83 1996
    296.3′11—dc20   96-23839
                                                   CIP

Manufactured in the United States of America. Jason Aronson Inc. offers books and cassettes. For information and catalog write to Jason Aronson Inc., 230 Livingston Street, Northvale, New Jersey 07647.

CONTENTS

INTRODUCTION

Nearly every religion is based on the existence of God or some Eternal Power. In Judaism, the God idea is central. "Hear O Israel, the Lord is our God, the Lord is One" has always represented the watchwords of our people.

Throughout history, the Jewish people have wrestled with various concepts of God—wondering, confronting, seeking, and finding God in many different ways. Grappling with these questions of God is a fundamental religious duty. Many people today are ill equipped to engage themselves seriously in theological issues and often avoid speaking about God altogether. Traditional Jews have been much more concerned with living according to God's commandments as given in the Torah and interpreted by rabbinic thinkers than with studying questions about God.

A great stumbling block for many people in making prayer a regular part of their lives is the question of God. Many are unsure of their beliefs. There are doubts, frustrations, and sometimes even hostilities. Grappling with fundamental questions about God is a religious duty.

One thing is certain. Nobody can know God in His full essence. There is no single universally accepted Jewish concept of God. The God of Jewish tradition is the God of the Bible, who shapes history, creates the world, and redeems the Jews from slavery. The God of rabbinic tradition resurrects the dead, and many of God's other powers are revealed in the prayer book. Almost everything written about God is conceptual images, metaphors, and symbols, and these continue to change with the inevitable changes that occur as civilization evolves.

This volume, an anthology on God, is intended to begin your exploration of Jewish approaches to the understanding of God. Although this is a book about God, it is more specifically a book about the ways in which Jews have spoken of and written about God through four thousand and more years of Jewish history. It will present ways in which the Bible, rabbinic literature, the prayer book, and sensitive theologians and philosophers have responded to questions about God and God's plan for the universe. This book is only intended as an introduction to the broad spectrum of issues concerning God. Hopefully it will serve as a catalyst for further study while assisting you in reclaiming your Jewish spiritual identity. Perhaps it will also assist you in working to develop a personal theology of your own.

God as a central category of discussion is returning in America. May this book challenge you to join in this discussion as you continue to grapple with theological issues.

1

Basic Conceptions of God

People throughout recorded history have conceived of God in a variety of different ways. The idea that the universe is created and governed by one Supreme Being is a much later development. This chapter will present an overview of the various known conceptions of God, beginning with the very earliest ones of primitive religion.

DYNAMISM: MANA

So-called primitive religion has a number of characteristic tendencies and common features. Many experts hold that prehistoric man's initial feeling for the Supernatural led him to think of it as a general, indefinable form of mysterious power found in almost everything. This belief is called dynamism, from the Greek *dynamis,* a power. The sacred is neither good nor bad in itself. It is also exceedingly dangerous to touch anything possessing this quality unless one knows how to handle it. Authorities have given this "power" the name "mana," which is the term used by the natives of Melanesia, the small islands north of New Guinea and Australia. Mana is a hidden force that attaches itself to persons or things and accounts for the success of an individual. For example, a canoe will not be swift unless mana sends it forward.

Mana is also dangerous and may bring the tribe incalculable injury. It is from this negative side of mana that we get the well-known idea of "taboo." It is forbidden to touch certain objects possessing mana: to touch them is "taboo," because of the terrible evils that might be unleashed. Only magicians were supposed to know how to control the mana and to prevent it from hurting the people.

ANIMISM

To primitive peoples, all of nature is pervaded by countless spirits, for it is not only persons or animals, but also the inanimate objects that have souls or spirits in them. This view is called "animism" (from the Latin *anima*—soul) and is still widespread among primitive peoples today.

Moved by awe and wonder of what they experienced, certain prehistoric peoples came to conceive of the Supernatural as something alive and inhabiting everything. Consequently, whatever happened became the work of "spirits," and all things, dead or alive, possessed such a living force or soul. For example, there was a spirit or soul in the tiger that people hunted. There was also a spirit in stones, bushes, and grasses.

Many remnants of animism have persisted until this day. Buddhists, for example, still revere the holy tree under which their teacher, Buddha, is said to have preached. Moslems venerate a large stone in the middle of their mosque in Mecca.

POLYTHEISM

The worship of many gods and goddesses is called polytheism. By the time the urban communities developed in the river valleys of the ancient world, polytheism was already an established view. Seven thousand years ago the Sumerians worshiped innumerable deities, including the stars and planet, sun and moon. It is quite likely that man first came to conceive of the Supreme Being as the sky deity. Being impressed with the ever-present heavens under whose favor or hostility he lived, it presented a mighty being to him. For several thousand years before the era of biblical prophecy was born, polytheism in one form or another was the type of religion that flourished.

It is important to note that to the polytheist, anything wonderful or mysterious was hailed as "godlike." Thus, gods were often immediately invented, named for the wonderful event, and then, should the wonder disappear, so also did the god.

Polytheism was never a serious threat to normative Judaism, because it is a form of idolatry, which could never be confused with biblical doctrine.

ANTHROPOMORPHISM

The Greeks used to present their many deities in human form. This was called "anthropomorphism" (from the Greek *anthropos*, a man, and *morphe*, form). In this way, they could better relate to and communicate with them, but not all ancient cultures anthropomorphized. The Celts preferred to use animals as symbols, while the Egyptians favored more abstract symbols, among which a well-known example is the solar disk, a symbol of their sun god.

HENOTHEISM

There was a strong tendency in polytheistic societies to recognize and exalt one of the gods above the others. That is to say, there would be a chief god—father of all of the gods. Thus, in Greek culture, for example, Father Zeus was the chief of the gods, considered stronger and more powerful than the others.

Sometimes one god could become the personification of the national spirit of a nationalistic people. When this occurred, the people had reached what is called "henotheism" (from the Greek *henos,* one, and *theos,* a god). This meant that they worshiped one god while also recognizing the existence of other gods. So-called henotheists always believed that their own god would triumph and reign supreme over all of the others.

KATHENOTHEISM

There was sometimes a tendency in polytheistic cultures for a person to worship each god in turn, as if, at any rate for the duration of the worship, there were no other god in the universe. This tendency has been called "kathenotheism," that is, the worship of one god at a time. Here the devotee takes each god individually and treats him or her as if he/she were the only god in the entire universe.

PANTHEISM

Pantheism (from the Greek *pantos,* all, and *theos,* god) is the doctrine that God is the totality of all existing things and that these in their totality are God. God is not a personal God, nor does God command people or seek their obedience. Consequently, there are almost no instances of pure pantheism within the normative Jewish tradition.

Pantheism received classic expression in India, which made possible its popularization by later generations of Buddhists and Hindus. Pantheism has also especially appealed to mystics, because these claim to experience a oneness with God. Much primitive thought is pantheistic in tendency. Some have even considered pantheism as the earliest philosophical expression of religion. Many of the Greek thinkers before Socrates, for instance, were pantheistic in outlook, regarding the universe as a living whole of which people are the parts.

DEISM

Deists refer to those who discovered that the many gods were but names for the One. They may see the deities as the imperfectly conceived aspects of a divinity that is personal and completely transcendent. In this view, God is not the All. God is the Source of all that is not He. God has created the universe, but takes no interest in it, having withdrawn Himself from the world. Deism thus eliminates all claims of Divine providence, miracles, and any form of intervention by God in history. Second, deism holds that all of the essential truths about

God are knowable by natural reason without any dependence on revelation. Numerous rabbinic texts attack the Greek philosophers who taught the doctrine of deism.

DUALISM

Dualism is the belief in both a good god and an evil god. In the Zoroastrian religion, for example, the good god, Ahura Mazda, is opposed by the evil one, Angra Mainyu, who in later times came to be called Shaitin (Satan). These two gods are eternally at war with one another. Ahura Mazda, the good god, was believed to be responsible for creating all the good things to be found in Iran. Angra Mainyu, on the other hand, created all bad things (disease, sickness, and so forth).

Dualism may take other forms as well. An Iranian called Mani (third century c.e.) taught a dualism of spirit and matter. The soul of a person is good, but it is in bondage to the contemptible matter that is his body. Only by denying the lusts of the body can a person overcome evil and regain the good.

Dualism was the only version of polytheism that made serious inroads into the cultural world of the Jews. As a response, the Talmud and Jewish liturgy constantly challenged the heresy of dualism.

AGNOSTICISM

T. H. Huxley coined the word "agnostic" to express his own state of mind. In his reading he learned of the "Gnostics," who had one thing in common. They all claimed a special "gnosis" (knowledge) of Divine truth. Generally speaking, they were also dualists who distinguished between the spiritual world of goodness and the material world of evil. The Gnostics claimed to know more about God than most people cared to claim. Huxley, however, claimed so much less of such knowledge that he thought the term "a-gnostic" would suit him better. Agnostics have come to be known as persons who do not categorically deny the existence of God, but rather deny that people could have any knowledge of God, who is beyond the realm of human comprehension.

THEISM

Theism recognizes that God transcends the universe, while at the same time, against deism, it recognizes God's immanence in the universe. It presents the paradox that God is both remote from the universe (position of deists) as well as near to people, allowing them to discover His values. To theists, the universe does seem to make sense, and the theist sees purpose in whatever direction he or she turns.

Classic theists in the main believe that:

1. God is one and alone.
2. God does not possess a body.
3. God is a spiritual Being that expresses love and concern for creation.
4. God is all-powerful and all-good.
5. God is omniscient.
6. God hears a person's prayers.

ATHEISM

An atheist is one who denies the existence of God. To many atheists, the universe simply does not seem to make sense. Atheism was known in the Middle Ages, and was often countered by various proofs for the existence of God that were common to all medieval philosophical theology. In modern times atheism has become a widely held doctrine, based on naturalistic scientific ideas.

NATURALISM

Naturalists deny that events or objects have any supernatural significance. For naturalists, scientific laws are adequate to account for all phenomena in life.

HUMANISM

In this philosophy, the dignity and worth of humans and their capacity for self-realization are emphasized, and supernaturalism is rejected. The goal of humanists is to develop one's power of reason in order to gain a better understanding of oneself, one's limitations, and one's capabilities. Self-realization is the highest virtue in humanistic religion.

TRINITY

The conception of God known as belief in the Trinity is especially associated with Christianity. Christian theologians normally interpret the Trinity as a doctrine of one God in three persons—the Father, Son, and Holy

Spirit. Jewish thinkers have rejected this doctrine of the Trinity as a denial of the Divine unity.

MONOTHEISM

Monotheism is the normative Jewish conception of God. It believes that God is the Creator and Sustainer of all things in the universe. God is the only Supreme Being, eternal and uncaused. God is a personal God who loves and commands humans. Many consider Abraham to be the founder of Israel's monotheism; hence in biblical and postbiblical tradition, God is frequently referred to as the God of Abraham, Isaac, and Jacob. The Jewish people have always been uncompromising monotheists, confessing their father in One God in prayer and in observances. Jewish monotheism connotes denial of Divine attributes to any other being.

2

CLASSICAL PROOFS FOR THE EXISTENCE OF GOD

It is quite likely that few people have ever become God believers because of any argument they have heard for the existence of God. It is more than likely that first of all they believed, and then sought an argument to justify their belief. And yet, the quest for an argument to prove the existence of God is natural enough.

Medieval Jewish philosophers in particular spent a considerable amount of time on the problems concerning the existence and nature of God.

The following is a brief summary of some of the classical proofs for the existence of God.

ONTOLOGICAL ARGUMENT (ARGUMENT FROM THE IDEA OF PERFECTION)

The ontological argument for the existence of God has been propounded by many theologians, including Anselm (1033–1109) and Descartes (1596–1650), two of its most notable. This argument goes something like this.

The existence of God is self-evident. Everyone really believes in God, though not everyone admits it. Everyone believes in God, because it is really impossible to do otherwise. For God is simply "a being than which nothing greater can be conceived."

Anselm argues that if the "x" (i.e., the greatest perfection of which one could conceive) exists only in his understanding, then it is still not the "x" than which nothing greater can be conceived. For Anselm, the "x" was not only in his understanding, but existed in itself, independent of anyone or anything else. The "x" therefore, was the Lord God.

COSMOLOGICAL ARGUMENT (ARGUMENT FROM "LOGICAL NECESSITY")

The so-called cosmological argument is very ancient. Its classic presentation dates back to the time of Aristotle (384–322 B.C.E.). It takes its starting point in the everyday world and is commonly presented as follows.

Everything that exists in the world of ordinary experience, such as a table, may very well not exist. That is to say, though such things certainly do exist, they do not exist of necessity. The table might very well never have been constructed. The existence of all such entities is what the exponents of this argument call "contingent" existence. But is there any other kind of existence? Does everything that actually exists have an existence of this kind, or is there some more "solid" kind of existence? The argument states that there must be some "ultimate" or "first" cause that does *necessarily* exist, and that first cause is what we know as God.

Jewish theologians demonstrate the existence of God using this type of proof with different examples. For instance, the medieval philosopher Maimonides uses the argument from motion. Since things in the world are in motion and no finite thing can move itself, every motion must be caused by another. But since this leads to an infinite regression, which is unintelligible, there must be an unmoved mover at the beginning of the series. This unmoved mover, the Prime Mover, is God, who possesses the power to move and make move without a preceding cause.

In Saadia Gaon's version of this argument, he deduces the existence of God from the creation of the world. He first demonstrates that the world must have been created in time out of nothing, and then he shows that such a world could only have been created by an omnipotent God whose essence is an absolute unity. This is another way of saying that everything in existence has a maker. It is reasonable to assume that the universe did not make itself either. Therefore, the existence of the universe implies a Creator.

TELEOLOGICAL ARGUMENT (ARGUMENT FROM APPARENT DESIGN OR PURPOSE)

Probably the most popular of all arguments to prove the existence of God has been the very ancient one called the Argument from Design. This is the Teleological Argument. The word "teleological" is from the Greek *telos,* an end. So a teleological universe is one that is ordered for the sake of an end or purpose.

The argument might run something as follows: Suppose you had never seen a watch and that you were to find one lying on the sands. All you could see in it would be a mechanical structure exhibiting an intricate adaptation of parts to one another. You would be likely to infer from this, however, that it was constructed by an intelligent being who designed this mutual adaptation in order to accomplish a certain end. But this (so runs the argument) is just what we encounter in the universe: order and design. And this Ultimate Designer is God.

MORAL ARGUMENT (ARGUMENT FROM THE EXPERIENCE OF VALUES, NOTABLY BUT NOT EX-CLUSIVELY ETHICAL OR MORAL VALUES)

The three previous proofs are all closely related. Some historians of philosophy have regarded them as variations of the Ontological, and others as variations of the Cosmological Argument. The usual objection to which they are usually exposed is that they are insufficient to communicate conviction to minds that are not already convinced. They lack compelling force.

The proof known as the Moral Argument is generally associated with the name of the eighteenth-century German philosopher Immanuel Kant. The argument would go something like this.

There is a good and there is a better, but there is no such thing as perfect (i.e., best) in earthly experience. Without the existence of a best, the concept of a good and better is imperfect. Therefore, the Perfect must lie beyond the earthly experience. This Perfect is God.

The Moral Argument has had great influence in the nineteenth and twentieth centuries. Standing apart from the previous trilogy of "logical" arguments, it is uniquely important in the development of thought on the subject. However, it is not, in the long run, any more assent compelling than the others. Indeed, one might ask: Is there really any conceivable argument that could prove the existence of anything in the mind of a person prepared to deny that existence?

3

GOD'S AUTHORITY: ORTHODOX, CONSERVATIVE, REFORM, AND RECONSTRUCTIONIST THEORIES OF REVELATION

The term revelation refers to an experience when God reveals His will to people. Revelation is what brings God into relationship with a community of people, and how it is understood is generally what distinguishes one religion from another.

The Bible understands revelation as an event, occurring at a specific time. In chapters 19 and 20 of the Book of Exodus, God reveals Himself to the entire Israelite community at Mount Sinai, presenting the commandments in the form of a covenant with the people. This revelatory experience at Mount Sinai is unique in that it takes place before an entire community of people—men, women, and children—who then act upon what they have seen and heard. "All that the Lord has spoken we will do" (Exodus 19:8) are words of commitment that future generations were to be bound with as well.

The exact manner of God's communication with the people is conceived differently by different groups of believers. Some will follow the biblical accounts of revelation literally, while others have understood it

more interpretively. The way in which people understand revelation will determine how they will subse-
quently deal with the issue of religious authority. Thus,
for example, if one believes in God and that the Torah is
the direct transcription of God's words, then the words
of the Torah become highly authoritative for that person. However, if one were to believe that human beings
wrote the Torah but were divinely inspired, then it may
be more possible for human beings to change the Bible's
laws and ideas when they find the need to do so.

This chapter will summarize the positions of the four
major streams of Judaism in America: Orthodox, Conservative, Reform, and Reconstructionist.

ORTHODOX VIEW

This traditional view maintains that God dictated the
words of the Torah to Moses, and Moses recorded those
words in one text called the *Chumash* (the Five Books
of Moses). Proponents of this view also hold that paral-
lel to this written text, God revealed the authentic
interpretation of this written Torah, called the Oral
Torah. This Oral Torah was transmitted orally from
generation to generation by the rabbinic authorities of
the first through the fifth centuries c.e. By the end of
the fifth century, the Jewish people had in their possession the complete, authoritative record of God's Will.

In this traditionalist view, whose exponents include
Rabbis Samson Raphael Hirsch, the founder of German
neo-Orthodoxy, Rabbi Eliezer Berkovits, and Rabbi
Norman Lamm (current president of Yeshiva University), God transmitted His will to the Israelites verbally

and in its entirety. This implies that the entire Torah is binding on the Jew in every detail, and the Torah is authoritative because it is the explicit word of God.

CONSERVATIVE VIEW

The nature of revelation and its meaning for the Jewish people have been understood in various ways within the Conservative community. Most Conservative theologians believe that the single greatest event in the history of God's revelation took place at Sinai, but was not limited to it. God's communication continued in the Prophets, the talmudic Rabbis, and remains alive today in the Jewish law codes.

The Conservative theologians have several positions relative to the nature of revelation:

1. In the first position are those who maintain that God dictated His will at Sinai and at other times as well. These revelations were written down by human beings thus resulting in the many sources of biblical literature. The revelation at Mount Sinai is the most public and authentic recording of God's will. Jewish law, however, is identified and determined by the ways in which each generation of rabbis interpreted and applied the law. In short, this position maintains that there was a verbal revelation at Mount Sinai, but unlike the traditionalist viewpoint, openly asserts that God's word was recorded by human beings. Exponents of this first position in Conservative Judaism include Abraham Joshua Heschel and Rabbi David Novak.

2. This viewpoint maintains that divinely inspired human beings wrote the Torah at various times and

places. Jewish law can therefore change because the Torah is a combination of both Divine inspiration and human articulation. These changes, however, can only be made through rabbinic decisions and communal custom. Exponents of this viewpoint include the twentieth-century American Rabbis Ben Zion Bokser and Rabbi Robert Gordis.

3. The advocates of this third position in Conservative Judaism assert that revelation is the disclosure of God Himself, but not the declaration of a specific set of rules and laws. The Torah, therefore, becomes the record of how human beings responded to God when they came into contact with Him. The Bible is simply the human recording of the encounter between man and God. Since people can and will continue to have encounters with God, the law may be changed to reflect the new understanding of God's will that results from those encounters. Changes in the law, however, can only be made by the Rabbis in behalf of the Jewish community, and never by individuals on their own. Exponents of this viewpoint include the British Rabbi Louis Jacobs and the late Rabbi Seymour Siegel, professor of philosophy at the Jewish Theological Seminary of America.

RECONSTRUCTIONIST VIEW

This view holds that human beings wrote the Torah, and there is no divinity ascribed to them. Nevertheless, Jewish law has authority for the Jewish people through its customs and folkways. Communal authorities in each generation can and must help individuals reconstruct Judaism with current meaningful customs and ideas. This viewpoint is the polar opposite of the traditionalist one, and its major exponent was Rabbi Mordecai Kaplan, founder of the Reconstructionist Movement, and Rabbi Ira Eisenstein, president of the Reconstructionist College.

REFORM VIEW

For many Reform theologians, the Torah is God's will written by human beings. As time goes on, people will come to understand God's will better and better. Sometimes called "progressive revelation," this theory maintains that each individual can be the recipient of revelation if he or she will only pay attention to the evidences of God and deduce from the nature and moral orders of the universe what God wants. Exponents of this viewpoint include Rabbi Eugene Borowitz, Professor of Theology at Hebrew Union College.

IN SUMMATION

Clearly the nature of revelation and its meaning for the Jewish people have been understood in different ways by the theologians of the four main streams of American Judaism. The Orthodox continue to maintain direct verbal revelation, affirming that God revealed His will at Sinai in both a written and an oral form (written down in the Talmud). Thus the texts of both the Bible and Talmud are understood as the exact word of God, making the laws highly authoritative, since they are in effect Divine.

For Conservative theologians, there is a range of possibilities, from the exponents of continuous revelation that hold that God dictated His will at Sinai and other times (and it was written down by human beings) to the exponents who held that the Torah is the human record of the encounter between God and the people at Sinai. In this latter view, it is believed that people continue to have encounters with God, and the law must be changed to reflect every new understanding of God's will.

Reconstructionist theologians claim no divinity for the Torah, maintaining that humans wrote the Torah. Communal authorities in every generation must help individuals reconstruct Judaism with meaningful customs that will meet the needs of the times.

Finally, Reform Judaism's progressive revelation maintains that the Torah is God's will written by human beings. Each individual decides both what and how to obey.

4

WRITING AND PRONOUNCING GOD'S NAME

Tradition relates that the name of God, consisting of the four letters *yod, hei, vav, hei*—was revealed to Moses at the burning bush. Its precise pronunciation was passed on to Aaron and kept a very closely guarded secret among the Priests, the religious functionaries of the time. This was done so that the people would never be able to use God's name irreverently. Only on one single occasion, that of Yom Kippur, the Day of Atonement, was the High Priest allowed to utter the real name of God. This was done during the confessional of sins on behalf of the people. When the priest uttered the holy name, his voice was lost in the singing of the other priests so that the Israelites would not be able to hear the secret pronunciation.

Outside of the ancient sanctuary, the term *Adonai* was used to connote God's name. Whenever the original four Hebrew letters are found in the Bible, or when God's name is called in prayer, it is pronounced *Adonai*. In ordinary conversation, however, the custom has arisen to call God *HaShem,* meaning "The Name," in order to protect God's name even further from possible misuse.

There are several Hebrew expressions signifying trust in God's dependability, which have been used by religious Jews regardless of the language that they are accustomed to speaking. The term *HaShem* comprises each of these expressions:

Baruch HaShem—Thank God: When a person wants to show gratitude for something in his or her life, that person will frequently use the expression of thankfulness *Baruch HaShem*. For example, when asked about his job, the person might answer *Baruch HaShem,* as if to say, thank God, I'm doing okay.

The phrase *Beezrat HaShem* means "with the help of God." Many traditional Jews will preface their plans or resolutions with this expression. In addition, when writing a letter, a traditionalist is likely to include the Hebrew letters *bet* and *hei* at the top on the right. These Hebrew letters begin each of the Hebrew words *beezrat hashem*.

Finally, the Hebrew phrase *im yirtzeh hashem* means "if it pleases God" or "if it is the will of God." This phrase is often used in connection with hopes and plans, and usually qualifies some activity. For example, a person might say, "I will see you next week, *im yirtzeh hashem*."

Rabbinic law (Talmud *Shavuot* 35a) states that it is forbidden to erase the name of God, and for that reason, care is taken not to write the Divine Name upon any document or paper that might be destroyed. If the Divine Name is written, it can only be discarded through ritual burial, similar to that of sacred texts and ritual items.

The restrictions against writing God's name, although usually applicable only to Hebrew names, have been extended by various rabbinic sources to include the writing of the name in the vernacular. Thus, one might find that the name of God is written as "G-d." In this way, one would protect himself against the possibility of writing the Divine Name in vain.

5

GOD IN THE BIBLE

A folkloristic tale tells of a wise person who tried to answer the question, "Who is God?" Month after month he thought about it, and finally he began to lose hope that he would ever find an answer.

One day, as he was taking a walk along the seashore, he saw children playing in the sand. They were digging deep holes and pouring water from the ocean into them. The man asked them what they were doing.

"We are emptying the ocean of water," one of the children replied.

The man said nothing, but smiled. "How foolish it is to try to empty the ocean of its water." But then his smile vanished, for he suddenly realized that he was as foolish as they were. For how could he, a human being with limited knowledge, hope to ever understand the true nature of God.

To know everything about God, including God's true essence, is an impossible task. The Bible, too, also came to a similar conclusion. As a collection of many volumes composed by different authors living in various countries over a period of more than a millennium, diverseness in presentation of the concept of God is to be expected. The Bible is a blend of the thoughts, beliefs, and intuitions of many generations into a single spiritual structure—the faith of Israel, at the heart of which lies the biblical idea of God. This section presents a cross-section of the divergent ideas about God as presented throughout the Bible that will help to shape a biblical composite view of God.

THE ONE INCOMPARABLE GOD

God is the Hero of the Bible. The entire narration is related to God and God's relationship to people. Nowhere in the Bible is there an offering of proof that God exists. The Bible begins by stating (Genesis 1:1) that "in the beginning, God created the heaven and the earth." It is apparent that the existence of God is taken for granted. Nowhere is it doubted. For the biblical Israelite, God is the only God. God is the beginning and the cause and creator of all things.

The high point of almost every Jewish worship service is one verse taken from the Bible. It is recited in both the evening and morning services, and also when the Torah scroll is taken out of the Ark.

"Hear O Israel, the Lord our God, the Lord is One" (Deuteronomy 6:4). God is the One and the only One. There are no other gods. Whereas other peoples of the ancient Near East believed that there were many gods,

Israel's God acted alone. At the time of creation, there was no other deity but God.

The second of the Ten Commandments also firmly establishes the singularity of God. God says (Exodus 20:2–3), "You shall have no other gods beside Me. You shall not make for yourself a sculptured image, or any likeness of what is in the heavens above, or on the earth below, or in the waters under the earth." This commandment demands recognition of God's singularity and forbids His presentation in any forms of sculptured image. In an ancient biblical world filled with myriads of deities, the simple truth of God's unity is demanded and proclaimed.

The Book of Isaiah reiterates and reaffirms the concept of God's singularity and uniqueness in these three passages:

Remember this and stand fast . . .
That I am God, and there is none else;
I am God, and there is none like Me!
(Isaiah 46:8–9)

Before Me no God was formed,
Nor shall there be any after Me.
I, I am the Lord,
And besides Me there is no savior.
(Isaiah 43:10–11)

I am the first and I am the last;
Besides Me there is no God.
(Isaiah 44:5)

GOD CREATES AND ACTS IN THE WORLD

God's power and wisdom find their ultimate expression in the work of creation. The universe is designed and executed by Divine decree. God speaks and things in the world come into being. For example, God said (Genesis 1:3) "let there be light, and there was light." All successive acts of creation in the first chapter of the Bible are presented in detail as God successively calls things into being.

Once the world was created, God also established a predictable order for it. "He made the moon to mark the seasons, the sun knows when to set" (Psalm 104:19).

Once again the Prophet Isaiah sums up God's distinctive characteristic of Creator in these words: "I am the Lord who made all things, who stretched out the heavens alone, and who spreads out the earth" (Isaiah 44:24).

GOD IS IMAGELESS

The biblical prohibition of sculptured images for purposes of adoration stresses the incorporeality of God. "You saw no shape when the Lord your God spoke to you at Horeb out of the fire," Deuteronomy (4:15) reminds the people. The second of the Ten Commandments further reiterates this theme: "You shall not make for yourself a sculptured image, or any likeness of what is in the heavens above, or on the earth below, or in the waters under the earth" (Exodus 20:4). Because God is invisible and spiritual, the Bible commanded that no person ought to make any statue or image that might be misunderstood as being a portrait of God.

It is true that the Bible often refers to God as if God did have a "body." This is especially the case in the sections of the Bible that are written in poetic form. For example, in the well-known Song at the Red Sea, we read the following: "Your right hand, O God, dashes into pieces the enemy" (Exodus 15:6). "And with the blast of Your nostrils the waters piled up" (Exodus 15:8). These images are generally to be understood poetically and metaphorically. A certain amount of figurative language (i.e., anthropomorphism) is built into human speech, and we cannot really dispense with it. This is done because of the limitations of human language in describing God. Thus the "strong right hand of God" is a symbol of God's power, as is "the blast of the nostrils of God."

Even Moses, who "knew" God "face to face" (Deuteronomy 34:10), was, according to the Bible, allowed to see only the "likeness of God" (Numbers 12:8). He was told that "you will see My back, but My face must not be seen" (Exodus 33:23). Many interpreters deduce from this passage the teaching that no living being can see God's face, that is, penetrate God's eternal essence. It is only from the *rearward* that we can "know" God.

In the remarkable revelatory experience at Mount Sinai, the Israelites hear God's voice but see no form: "God spoke to you out of the fire; you heard the sound of words, but perceived no shape—nothing but a voice" (Deuteronomy 4:12).

The composite message of the Bible is that God has no likeness, and no one will ever truly know what God looks like. It is possible, though, to "feel" God's Presence, but that is as close as humanity can ever expect to come.

GOD HAS MANY NAMES

What is important to any culture is often called by many different words or descriptions. For example, Eskimos have a variety of different names for "snow." People who live in the desert have many different names for "camel." It is therefore not surprising that the Bible has a variety of names for God, each revealing a different aspect of God's essence. Here is a brief summary of the names of God as they appear in the Bible.

1. *El*: This is the oldest Semitic term for God. Rarely used as a personal name for God, *El* is an appellative, often used in combination with other names for God. For example, *El Olam* (Eternal God) is used in Genesis 21:33: "Abraham planted a tamarisk tree in Beersheba and called there on YHVH (Lord), *El Olam* (the Eternal God)." Or in Exodus 6:3, God is referred to as *El Shaddai* (God Almighty). In Genesis 16:13, Sarah drives away Hagar and she flees into the western Negev. There at a well she has a vision of God, "and she called YHVH who spoke to her, 'You are *El Roi*—a Seeing God.' " The Divine Name *El Brit* (God of the Covenant) appears only in the book of Judges (9:46), where mention is made of the "house of *El Brit* at Shechem."

The word *El* appears in many theophoric names, including those of *El*isha, *El*ijah, Isra*el*, Ishma*el*, and Samu*el*.

2. *Elohim*: *Elohim* is the general designation of the Divine Being in the Bible, as the fountain and source of all things. *Elohim* is a plural form, which is often used in Hebrew to denote plenitude of might. The word *Elohim* appears in the opening verse of the Bible "In

the beginning, God (*Elohim*) created the heaven and the earth" (Genesis 1:1).

The biblical theory (known as the Documentary Hypothesis) holds that the Bible, instead of a book produced by God through Moses (a traditionalist view), was the product of various groups of people who gathered and edited collections of material. These people were often called "schools" of writers and editors. One of the schools was called the E school because its contributions used the Hebrew *Elohim* when referring to God. According to the Documentary Hypothesis, this school developed its biblical source material from about 750 B.C.E. to 650 B.C.E.

In Jewish mysticism, *Elohim* has come to represent the quality of *din* (stern judgment) or *gevurah* (power), and serves as a balance to El's free-flowing love. The Patriarch Isaac has come to symbolize this aspect since he voluntarily submitted himself to be bound and offered as a sacrifice to God.

3. *YHVH*: Another ancient biblical name for God was YHVH, probably pronounced Yahweh. The consensus of scholarly opinion today is that YHVH derived from a form of the verb "to be" used in a causative sense. Christians, who tried reading this name for God with the vowels now appearing with it in the Hebrew text, came up with the name "Yehovah," often commonly pronounced "Jehovah."

According to the Documentary Hypothesis, the first school of writers and editors to gather and assemble the oral traditions and experiences of the Israelites was the J School (850 B.C.E.), named after the name of God, JHVH, which appears in the writings of this first school. This name for God was "announced" for the first time by

Moses in the Book of Exodus (6:3): "I appeared to Abraham, Isaac and Jacob as El Shaddai (God Almighty) but I did not make Myself known to them by My name YHVH—the Lord." The name "YHVH" appears in other places of the Bible as well. For example, in the Book of Genesis (14:22), Abram said to the King of Sodom: "I have lifted up my hand to YHVH . . ."

Though the biblical Israelites might have known how to pronounce this name of God correctly, in reality we do not know how to pronounce it, since in ancient times Hebrew did not use vowels and the Bible provides no clues as to its proper pronunciation. Only the High Priests, on the Day of Atonement, inside the Jerusalem Temple's Holy of Holies, would be permitted actually to recite this name for God and thereby expiate the sins of all Israel. Fearing that this name of God might be misused or mispronounced, a group of scribes called the Masoretes decided that this name for God should be read as *Adonai* (Lord).

In Jewish mysticism, YHVH represents the aspect of *tiferet* (beauty) or *rachamim* (compassion). It is the heart of the system, which receives the flow from above and channels it out to the worlds below. Jacob, Israel's third patriarch, is the personification of this quality.

4. *El Shaddai*: This Divine Name is frequently found in the Bible and is usually interpreted as "Almighty," derived from the prefix *she* (who) and *dai* (enough). Some say that its original is from the Akkadian word *sadu,* meaning mountain, in which case it would mean "God of the Mountain." Others say that it is also derived from the Arabic *shada,* which means "to heap benefits," and "to reconcile persons at enmity with one another."

This idea of beneficence and peace is amply borne out by the passages in Genesis in which "Shaddai" occurs (Genesis 17:1, 28:3, and 44:14). The meaning conveyed by them is that of Friend and Protector, who watches over the Patriarchs and bestows upon them and their descendants great material good.

The word *Shaddai* is again recorded in Exodus 6:3, as God reveals this name to Moses. It also appears in several other books of the Bible and numerous times in the Book of Job.

In mysticism, *El Shaddai* is associated with the quality of *netzach* (victory) and is often personified by Moses who led the Israelites to victory from Egypt.

The word *Shaddai* often appears too on the front of the *mezuzah* receptacle. Here its meaning has often been understood as an acronym for *Shomer Delatot Yisrael*—"Guardian of Israelite Doors."

Several biblical names include the word *Shaddai* within them. Examples of this are *Tzurishaddai* (Numbers 1:6), *Shedeur* (Numbers 1:5), and *Ammishaddai* (Numbers 1:12).

5. *Adonai*: Derived from the Hebrew *Adon* (lord), *Adonai* originally meant "my Lord" but has come to mean simply "the Lord." Although it is used as a name for God in and of itself, it is more frequently used as the euphemism for YHVH in liturgical settings or in the ritual readings of sacred texts.

Adonai as "Lord of all the earth" (Joshua 3:1) has a sovereign connotation to it and in mysticism is associated with the quality of *malchut* (majesty). This Divine Name is often personified by King David, a scion of the messianic line.

6. *Yah*: A short form of the Divine Name, *Yah* may represent the original form from which YHVH was expanded. *Yah* occurs in several places in the Bible, including Exodus 15:2 ("*Yah* is my strength and salvation") and Exodus 17:16 ("And he said: 'The hand upon the throne of *Yah*' "). It also appears in proper biblical names such as Elijah ("Eli*ya*hu" in Hebrew) and in the doxology, "Hallelujah" (Praise the Lord) (see Psalm 150).

7. ***Adonai Tzevaot***: "Lord of Hosts" is the traditional translation of this Divine Name. Some say that it probably means "He who brings the angelic hosts into being." This Divine Name appears in the famous verse in the Book of Isaiah (6:3), "Holy is 'Adonai Tzevaot,' the whole earth is filled with God's glory."

As a quality, *Adonai Tzevaot* is represented in mystic tradition by *hod* (grandeur) and is personified by Aaron the Priest whose responsibility it was to orchestrate the dramatic ritual and ceremony surrounding the service of God.

8. ***Other Divine Epithets***: Besides the above-mentioned Divine Names, there are other appellatives that are descriptive of God's nature. Here are ten descriptive names of God. These names stress God's creative ability, God's transcendent sanctity, God's sovereignty, God's loving-kindness, and God's dependability and great strength:

  i. *Konay shamayim ve'aretz*—Maker of heaven and earth (Genesis 14:19).
  ii. *Boray Yisrael*—Creator of Israel (Isaiah 43:15).
  iii. *Kadosh*—the Holy One (Isaiah 40:25).
  iv. *Roi*—My Shepherd (Psalm 23:1).
  v. *Ro'eh Yisrael*—Shepherd of Israel (Psalm 80:2).

vi. *Tzur*—The Rock (Deuteronomy 32:4).

vii. *Melech Yisrael*—King of Israel (Isaiah 44:6).

viii. *Abir Yisrael*—Mighty One of Israel (Isaiah 1:24).

ix. *Yozter*—Creator (Isaiah 29:16).

x. *Ehyeh asher Ehyeh*—I am that I am (Exodus 3:14).

GOD AND GOD'S CHOSEN PEOPLE

The idea that the Israelites were specially selected by God to carry out God's purposes is prominent in the Bible. Numerous passages deal with the so-called chosen people theme. One of the first is the mention of the Israelites as specially elected by God. God says to Abraham (Genesis 12:1–3) "Get out of your country . . . and go into the land that I will show you and I will make of you a great nation and I will bless you and make your name great."

According to a second story in the Bible, God chose Israel to be His special people when God led them out of Egypt and gave them the Torah on Mount Sinai: "You have seen what I did to the Egyptians and how I bore you on eagles' wings and brought you to Me. Now, therefore, if you will listen to Me and keep My covenant, then you shall be My own treasure from all peoples; for all the earth is Mine. And you shall be to Me a Kingdom of Priests and a Holy Nation" (Exodus 19:4–6).

Two additional verses from the Five Books of Moses illustrate God's conditions for His special choice of the Israelites as God's chosen ones. Israel was to be God's own special vehicle for His purposes, but this singling

out was not based on a special merit of the Israelites:
". . . God has chosen you to be God's treasure from all
of the peoples that are upon the face of the earth. God
did not set His love upon you, nor choose you, because
you were more in number than any other people—for
you were the fewest of all peoples—but because God
loved you" (Deuteronomy 7:6-8).

"Behold, unto God belongs the heavens, and the
heaven of heavens, the earth, with all that is therein.
Only God had a delight in your ancestors to love them
and God chose their seed after them, even you, above
all peoples, as it is this day" (Deuteronomy 10:14-15).

Israel's chosenness, according to the Prophet Amos,
did not give them special privileges. Rather, it imposed
additional obligations and commitment upon them. As
the Prophet Amos (3:2) states: "You alone have I singled
out of all of the families of the earth. That is why I will
call you to account for all of your transgressions."

The nature of the relationship between Israel and
God underwent a further development during the
Babylonian Exile. It was then that the Prophet Isaiah
pointed out that God's close relationship with the
Israelites also imposed a special mission upon them.
The Israelites were told that they will perform their
mission not simply by telling the word of God and
God's righteous demands to the nations of the world,
but by living them. In this way, Israel will be "a light
unto the nations":

I am the Lord, I have called you in righteousness,
I have taken you by the hand and kept you;
For I have given you as a covenant to the people,

For a light unto the nations,
To open the eyes that are blind,
To bring out the prisoners from the dungeon,
From the prison those who sit in darkness. . .
(Isaiah 42:6–7)

Hence, as the chosen people, Israel has not been singled out by God for special privileges and rewards, but rather for special responsibilities to humankind.

GOD'S ATTRIBUTES

As the Israelites grew impatient with Moses who had ascended Mount Sinai, they built a Golden Calf and danced around it. Moses upon his descent was horrified by what he saw, and shattered the Ten Commandments at the foot of Mount Sinai. Sometime thereafter Moses again ascended Mount Sinai a second time, and prostrated himself in prayer before God. After forty days, he returned to the Israelites, when, in addition to new tablets of law, he brought a Heavenly commentary on that law, the thirteen attributes of the Divine Nature:

"The Lord, the Lord God, merciful and gracious, long-suffering, and abundant in goodness and truth. Keeping mercy to the thousandth generation, forgiving iniquity and transgression and sin, and clears [the guiltless]" (Exodus 34:6–7).

Although there are not literally an enumeration of thirteen attributes in these two verses, rabbinic interpretation has understood them as such. The repetition of the Lord's name has come to be understood to signify that God is merciful to one about to sin but not yet guilty of sinning, and to the sinner who has repented. This represents the first two Divine qualities. The third attribute of God is inferred from the Hebrew word *El,* meaning powerful to act as His wisdom dictates. The term merciful (*rachum*) has come to be understood to denote that God acts like a parent to his children, preventing them from falling (i.e., the fourth attribute).

The fifth attribute: God is gracious (*channun*) to assist those who have fallen and cannot rise. The sixth attribute: God is slow to anger, patient and hopeful that the transgressor will repent.

The seventh attribute: God is abounding in kindness, both to the righteous person as well as to the wicked. The eighth: God is truthful and faithful to carry out His promises. The ninth: God extends mercy to thousands of generations, placing the merits of the fathers to the credit of the children. The tenth: God forgives all iniquity, sins committed with premeditation. The eleventh: God pardons all transgressions, sins committed in a spirit of rebellion. The twelfth: God forgives sins committed inadvertently. The thirteenth: God acquits those who repent.

The thirteenth attribute, as understood by the Rabbis, is not a true rendition of the biblical passage that assures that God "will by no means clear the guilty." However, the Rabbis who developed the understanding of these attributes wanted to underscore God's quality of mercy over that of strict justice. Hence, they took the first word of the phrase (*venakkeh*—will clear) and omitted the other two words (i.e., *lo yenakkeh*—will not clear), to conform with their theme of God's mercy and compassion.

These Divine qualities, as portrayed in the Bible, are not an attempt to describe the essence of God philosophically, but rather to represent God as the Source of all ethical behavior. God's attributes are to become the standard of a person's morality. It is also important to note that these verses comprising the thirteen attributes of God are recited in synagogue before the opening of the Holy Ark on all holidays, except when the holiday falls on a Sabbath. It has been said that the recitation of these attributes at this juncture in the service originated in the time of the Middle Ages under the influence of the famous mystic Isaac Luria.

GOD'S PROPHETS

Throughout the biblical period, prophets were chosen by God to serve as His "mouthpiece." Abraham was the first person in the Bible to be referred to as a prophet: "But you must restore the man's wife—since he is a prophet" (Genesis 20:7). Moses was called a prophet twice in the Bible: "The Lord your God will raise up for you a prophet from among your own people like myself; him you shall heed" (Deuteronomy 18:15). "Never again did there arise in Israel a prophet like Moses, whom the Lord singled out, face to face . . ." (Deuteronomy 34:10).

Although Moses was a man who spoke for God in a special way, he was much better known as the facilitators of the Israelites from Egyptian bondage.

There were fifteen literary prophets in Israel, whose careers covered nearly four centuries, beginning about 750 B.C.E. They were called the literary prophets either

because they wrote down their prophecies or because
we have books in the Bible named after them. Most of
these prophets were chosen by God in times of social or
political crisis in Israel, and prophesied in relation to
specific events that either had taken place or were about
to occur. They all had the ability to predict what would
happen to the Israelite people if they followed a certain
course of action.

Hosea, considered a minor prophet because his book
was quite short, begged the Israelites to change their
corrupt ways:

> Hear the word of the Lord
> O people of Israel.
> For the Lord has a case
> Against the inhabitants of this land,
> Because there is no honesty and goodness
> And no obedience to God in the land.
> False swearing, dishonesty, and murder,
> And theft and adultery are rife;
> Crime follows upon crime. (Hosea 4:1–2)

Most if not all of the prophets of Israel were passionate believers in life. Each prophet reiterated the theme
that God takes no delight in destroying the evildoer.
More than anything else, God only wanted humanity to
turn away from its corrupt ways and return to God so
that humanity might live and not die.

The prophet Ezekiel put it this way: "Cast all the
transgressions by which you have offended, and get
yourselves a new heart and a new spirit, that you may
not die, O House of Israel. For it is not My desire that

anyone shall die—declares God. Repent, therefore, and live!'' (Ezekiel 18:31–32).

Similarly, the Prophet Jeremiah in his well-known parable of the potter and the clay makes this same sentiment very clear:

> O House of Israel, can I not deal with you like this potter? says the Lord. Just like clay in the hands of the potter, so are you in My hands, O House of Israel! At one moment I may decree that a nation or a kingdom shall be uprooted and pulled down and destroyed; but if that nation against which I made the decree turns back from its wickedness, I change My mind concerning the punishment I planned to bring on it. And now, say to the men of Judah and the people of Jerusalem: Thus said the Lord: I am devising disaster for you and laying plans against you. Turn back, each of you, from your wicked ways, and mend your ways and your actions. (Jeremiah 18:6–8;11)

The Prophets, as mouthpieces for God, were often scornful of the Israelites' belief that they were acting in a religious way by simply bringing sacrifices to the Temple. On the contrary, what was important to God was that ritual led to ethical living. Here now are the famous words of the Prophet Micah:

> With what shall I approach the Lord,
> Do homage to God on high?
> Shall I approach God with burnt offerings,

With calves of a year old?
Would the Lord be pleased with thousands of rams
With myriads of streams of oil?
Shall I give my firstborn for my transgression,
The fruit of my body for my sins?
He has told you, O man, what is good,
And what the Lord requires of you:
Only to do justice and to love goodness
And to walk humbly with your God. (Micah 6:6–8)

From this statement we learn that the God of Israel requires ethical behavior of human beings. Ritual that does not lead to good behavior is of no use to God.

JUSTICE AND MERCY OF GOD

Central among the biblical affirmations about God are those that emphasize God's justice and righteousness on the one hand, and God's mercy and lovingkindness on the other. God's justice and mercy are both affirmed in God's proclamation to Moses at Sinai before the giving of the Ten Commandments: "The Lord, the Lord, a God compassionate and gracious, slow to anger, abounding in kindness and faithfulness, extending kindness to the thousandth generation, forgiving iniquity, transgression and sin. Yet God does remit all punishment, but visits the iniquity of the fathers upon the children and children's children, upon the third and fourth generations" (Exodus 34:6–7).

Justice and mercy are the bases of the covenant between God and the Israelites. God's mercy is revealed in the fact that He redeemed the Israelites from Egyptian slavery to make them His covenantal people: "When Israel was a child, I loved him, out of Egypt I called my son" (Hosea 11:1). God's justice is revealed in the fact that God punishes the Israelites if they sin and do not follow God's covenant: "You only have I known of all the families of the earth. Therefore I will punish you with all your transgressions" (Amos 3:2).

Both the aspects of justice and mercy are also evident in the Bible's portrayal of God's "marriage" with Israel: "I will betroth you to me in righteousness and justice, in steadfast love and in mercy" (Hosea 2:19). In exercising His justice and punishing the Israelites when they do sin, God reveals His great power. God's justice, however, is frequently tempered by His mercy: "My heart recoils within me, My compassion grows warm and tender. I will not execute My fierce anger, I will not again destroy Ephraim" (Hosea 11:8–9).

In summation, the relationship between justice and mercy in God's attitude toward the Israelites is quite varied. Some verses emphasize God's mercy, whereas others emphasize God's justice.

GOD AND EVIL

One of the important assumptions in the Bible is that God rewards goodness and punishes the wicked. For example, the Book of Deuteronomy reminds us:

If you listen diligently to God's commandments, which I command you this day, to love the Lord your God, and to serve Him with all your heart and all of your soul, I will give the rain of your land in its

season, the former rain and the latter rain . . . And I
will give grass in your fields for your cattle, and you
shall eat and be satisfied. Be careful, lest your heart
be deceived, and you turn aside and worship other
gods. And the anger of God be kindled against you,
and He shut up the heaven, so that there shall be no
rain, and the ground shall not yield her fruit, and
you shall perish quickly from off the good land
which God gives you. (Deuteronomy 11:17)

In this example above, both the rewards and punishments are agricultural, referring to rainfall, which was
and still is a matter of life and death in the Land of Israel.
This doctrine is bound up with the biblical belief that
God is a God of Justice, and because God is just, God
will not treat the righteous and the wicked in the same
manner. In some way, it must be better with the former
than with the latter, through the justice of God.

Later, in the Book of Psalms (37:25) we read the
following; "I have been young and now I am old, but I
have never seen a righteous man abandoned or his
children seeking bread." And again, in Psalms 92:8, 13,
14: "Though the wicked spring up as grass, though all
evil-doers blossom, it is only that they may be destroyed forever. . . ." "The righteous shall flourish like
a palm tree, thriving like a cedar in Lebanon. . . ."

From time to time, however, we see in the Bible that
the innocent often suffer for the sins of others, and that
the wicked are not always punished nor are good people always rewarded. The first time this issue is raised is
when God is about to destroy the cities of Sodom and
Gomorrah for the sin that has come to be rabbinically

interpreted as sexual perversion. Abraham challenges God's Divine justice with these well-known words: "Shall not the Judge of all the earth do right?" (Genesis 18:25).

Moses, five centuries later, echoes a similar cry in another context (i.e., the Israelites find themselves enslaved under Egyptian sovereignty): "O God, why have You done evil to this people" (Exodus 5:22).

The Israelite prophets are no less perplexed, as Jeremiah asks: "Why does the way of the wicked prosper? Why do all who are treacherous thrive?" (Jeremiah 12:1).

The Book of Job is, almost in its magnificent entirety, a struggle to solve the problem of unwarranted human suffering. It ultimately concludes that human beings are unable to understand God's ways, "Who can understand the thunder of God's mighty deeds?" (Job 26:14).

In the final analysis, the Bible calls for faith: "But the righteous shall live by his faith" (Habakkuk 2:4). "Those who wait for the Lord shall renew their strength" (Isaiah 40:31).

GOD'S ANGELS

Angels are an ancient element in Jewish tradition, first appearing in some of the earliest passages of the Bible. Then they appear sporadically throughout the Bible in a variety of places.

For the most part, biblical angels are messengers conveying the Divine commands and promises, rewards and punishments. They are sometimes regarded as superhuman beings dwelling in heaven, who form the

Divine council and choir of God. Occasionally, however, they assume human form and reveal to man God's will and execute God's judgments.

In one of the truly great tests of faith, God commanded Abraham to offer his favorite son Isaac as a burnt offering. Abraham takes Isaac to the designated spot, and places him on the altar with the wood. Then, when he picks up a knife to actually slay his son, he is interrupted by an angel of God:

> Then the angel of the Lord called to him from Heaven: "Abraham, Abraham . . . Do not raise your hand against the lad . . . For now I know that you fear God, since you have not withheld your son, your favored one from Me. (Genesis 22:11–13)

The message of God's angel offers the key to understanding the theme of this story. The angel's message was that God does not want killing of people done in His name. This was a very different practice from that of the pagan world of the time, when human sacrifice was widely practiced.

In yet another story of the last of the three biblical patriarchs, Jacob transports his family and herd across the Jabbok river. There he encounters an angel with whom he wrestles:

> Jacob was left alone. And a man wrestled with him until the break of dawn. When he saw that he had not prevailed against him, he wrenched Jacob's hip at its socket, so that the socket of his hip was strained as he wrestled with him. Then he said, "Let me go, for dawn is breaking." But he an-

swered, "I will not let you go unless you bless me."
The other said, "What is your name?" He replied,
"Jacob." Said he, "Your name shall no longer be
called Jacob, but Israel, for you have striven with
divine and human beings and have prevailed."
Jacob asked, "Pray tell me your name." But he said:
"You must not ask my name." And he took leave of
him there. (Genesis 32:25–30)

Early rabbinic literature identified this angel as the
Archangel Gabriel. This angel's Hebrew name is synonymous with *gevurah,* the Hebrew word for power.
Gabriel appears as a sparring partner to help Jacob face
the potential disaster at daybreak. As a result of Jacob
prevailing, Gabriel responded by telling Jacob that he
had earned a new name—"Israel," meaning champion
of God.

In one of the most amazing chapters in the entire
Bible, an angel of God appears to Moses in a bush that is
not consumed:

An angel of the Lord appeared to him in a blazing
fire out of the bush. He gazed, and there was a bush
afire, yet the bush was not consumed. Moses said,
"I must turn aside to look at this wondrous sight.
Why does the bush not burn up?" When the Lord
saw that he had turned aside to look, God called to
him out of the bush: "Moses, Moses." He answered: "Here I am." And God said: "Do not
come closer. Remove your sandals from your feet,
for the place on which you stand is holy ground."
(Exodus 3:1–5)

Here we see that although an angel of God first appeared to Moses in the burning bush, God Himself eventually spoke to Moses directly and gave him His directive. The angel of the Lord is the spiritual being that draws Moses' attention to the voice of God.

In later books of the Bible, angels continue to make appearances. Joshua (5:13–15) has a vision of an angel disguised as a man, reminding him as the successor of Moses to be strong and of great courage. Gideon the Judge has an important encounter with God's angel who reminds him of his Divine mission with these words: "Go in this strength of yours and deliver Israel from the Midianites. I herewith make you my messenger" (Judges 6:14).

In the Book of Daniel, a new phenomenon emerges with respect to angels. None of the angels in the Hebrew Bible up to this point had a name. They were messengers of God, with no personal identity of their own. In the Book of Daniel, two angels are designated by name: Michael and Gabriel. Both are guardian angels whose purpose is to protect the Children of Israel. They also depicted events of the future that helped to brighten the minds of the Jewish people during the dark Maccabean era.

IN SUMMATION

We have seen that the Bible contains some very different ideas about God, but no single notion of God exists. God is One and Only, Creator of the world. Unlike the gods of other ancient Near East peoples, God has no female counterpart, nor does God have a wife, father, mother, son, or daughter. Although God has many names, each manifests a different attribute of God's nature. Both God's qualities of justice and mercy permeate the Bible, and God often tempers His justice with compassion and mercy. The God of Israel also puts a heavy emphasis on the importance of ethical behavior over pure ritual. Finally, God remains imageless with no person able to see God's likeness. God's special covenantal relationship with the Israelites permeates the Bible, and even when the Israelites fail to carry out their part of the covenant, God continues to assure them that the loving contractual covenant established at Mount Sinai will continue to last forever. In fact, this covenant was made not only with generations past, but also with the generations of all Israelites yet to come: "I make this covenant, with its sanctions, not with you alone but both with those who are standing here with us this day before the Lord our God and with those who are not with us here this day" (Deuteronomy 29:13–14).

6

GOD IN RABBINIC LITERATURE

Rabbinic literature was intended to enhance and interpret the biblical text, which often needed additional explanation and amplification. With regard to its understanding of God, it embellishes its understanding of the Israelite God with imagery and parable. Rabbinic literature includes the Talmud, in which are collected the records of academic discussion and judicial administration of Jewish law by generations of scholars during several centuries after 200 C.E. The Talmud consists of the Mishnah together with the Gemara, a commentary on the Mishnah.

The compilation of rabbinic works known as the Midrash refers to legal commentaries on the laws of the Bible as well as homiletical material for purposes of moral edification.

Similar to the Bible, rabbinic literature contains many statements and references to God, but no systematized discussion that deals exclusively with theology (i.e., the study of God). There is a general consensus, however, with regard to how the Rabbis viewed God. Here are some examples of rabbinic statements related to God that are intended to help form a composite view of how the Rabbis understood God.

GOD IS ONE AND ONLY

The recognition of the oneness of God is regarded by rabbinic scholars as a cardinal principle of Judaism, concerning which mankind as a whole was commanded, the seven precepts binding upon Noachians including idolatry. In a famous statement in the Midrash on the Book of Psalms (149:1), the Rabbis emphasized the unity and oneness of God:

> An earthly king is wont to have dukes and viceroys, who share with him in the burden of rule, and also have a share in the honor with which he is honored, but God is not so. He has no duke or governor or lieutenant. No other with Him does His work, but He does it alone. No other bears the burden with Him, but He bears it alone.

The Rabbis also tried to emphasize that in spite of the varieties of metaphor with which God is spoken of in the Bible, God is always the same God, the One and Only God: "God said to Israel, 'Because you have seen me in many likenesses, there are not therefore many gods. But it is ever the same God: I am the Lord your God'" (*Pesikta Kahana* 109b, 110a).

Numerous anti-Christian polemics are found throughout rabbinic literature. For example: "Rabbi Abbahu said: An earthly king has a father, a brother or a son. With God it is not so. For God says, 'I am the first, for I have no father; I am the last, for I have no brother; and there is no

God beside Me, for I have no son' '' (*Exodus Rabbah,* Yitro 29:5).

Finally, the Rabbis raised these Deuteronomic words "Hear O Israel, the Lord our God, the Lord is One" to a confession of faith. They ordained that these words be repeated by the entire body of worshipers when the Torah is taken out on Sabbaths and Festivals, in the Sanctification prayer (i.e., the *Kedusha*) on these occasions, after the *Neila* service as the culmination of the Day of Atonement, and in a person's last hour, when he or she was about to die. Even in private prayer, the Rabbis spared no effort to enhance the solemnity of its utterance. They proclaimed that the words of the *Shema Yisrael* must be said audibly, they ordained that the ear must hear what the lips utter, and they also stated that the last word in Hebrew, *echad* meaning One, was to be pronounced with special emphasis. All thoughts other than God's unity, they said, must be shut out, and the *Shema* must be spoken with total concentration of heart and mind. They further wrote that the reading of the *Shema* could not even be interrupted to respond to the salutation of a king.

GOD'S EXISTENCE CAN BE PROVEN

Although the Rabbis took the existence of God as a fundamental principle of Judaism without the need for proof, there were, on occasions, opportunities presented to them to prove the existence of God to others. Here is one example from the Midrash (*Temurah, Bet HaMidrash* 1:113–114):

Once someone knocked on the door of Rabbi Akiba's House of Study.

"Enter," said the Rabbi. The person who entered was a total stranger, who did not wear the traditional ritual fringes nor did he have a long beard like that of the Jew. His haircut was a Roman style one.

The stranger said, "I have a question for you. Who created the world?"

"God, the Holy One, created the world," answered Akiba.

"Prove it to me," the stranger said.

Akiba replied: "Come back tomorrow."

After the stranger left, Akiba resumed his teaching. When his students asked him what he would say to the stranger when the next day came, Akiba answered, "Wait and you will see!"

The stranger returned the following day and knocked on Rabbi Akiba's door.

"Come in," said Rabbi Akiba. "Today I have a question for you. What is it that you are wearing?"

"It's a robe," answered the stranger.

"Who made it?" inquired Akiba.

"The weaver," answered the stranger.

"Prove it to me," said Akiba.

"How preposterous," answered the stranger. "Can you not tell just by looking at the garment and the design that this is the work of a weaver?"

"And can't you tell just by looking at the world, that it is the work of God?" asked Rabbi Akiba.

The stranger looked dumbfounded. He had nothing more to say to Akiba, and left the House of Study.

Akiba then turned to his students and explained, "Just as a house was obviously built by a builder, and a garment sewn by a tailor, so the world was obviously made by God, the Creator of all."

GOD IS OMNIPRESENT

The Rabbis stressed throughout rabbinic literature that God was not limited to the Temple. Even as God was in the Temple, so God is also present in the synagogues in which Israelites pray:

God says, "Who has ever come into a synagogue, and has not found My glory there?" "And not only that," said Rabbi Aibu, "but if you individually are in a synagogue, God stands by you." [Psalm 82] (*Deuteronomy Rabbah, Ki Tavo* 7:2)

"My love is like a gazelle." [Song of Songs, 9] As the gazelle leaps from place to place, and from fence to fence, and from tree to tree, so God jumps from synagogue to synagogue to bless all of the children of Israel. (*Numbers Rabbah, Naso* 11:2)

The Rabbis emphasized the importance of the administration of justice as a holy act and as a way of bringing God into the presence of students: "When three sit and judge, the Shechinah is in their midst" (Talmud *Berakhot* 6a).

GOD AND THE HUMAN SOUL
HAVE MANY SIMILARITIES

The comparison of the relation of God to the world with the relation of the soul to the body is frequent in rabbinic literature. For instance:

> As God fills the whole world, so also the soul fills the whole body. As God sees, but cannot be seen, so also the soul sees, but cannot be seen. As God nourishes the whole world, so also the soul nourishes the whole body. As God is pure, so also the soul is pure. As God dwells in the innermost part of the Universe, so also the soul dwells in the innermost part of the body. (Talmud *Berakhot* 10a)

> And in another example: It is written, "Praise the Lord, O my soul" [Psalm 103:1]. Why did David think of praising God with his soul? He said, "The soul fills the body and God fills the world" [Jeremiah 23:24], so let the soul which fills the body praise God who fills the world. (*Leviticus Rabbah, Vayikra* 4:8)

GOD AND THE ANGELS

The Rabbis of old frequently made reference to the angels and certainly believed that they existed. They seem to have little religious importance, and were not often objects of adoration. The Rabbis seemed to prefer that people communicate directly to God rather than using angels as intermediaries, and never wanted people to confuse the angels for God Himself: "If a person is in distress, let him not call on Michael or Gabriel but let him call directly on Me, and I will listen to him immediately'' (Jerusalem Talmud, *Berakhot* 9:1).

On occasion, we find legendary stories related to the visitation of angels to the homes of Jewish people. Here is a famous example of such a legend, upon which the Friday evening prayer *Shalom Aleichem* (a prayer welcoming the angels) is based:

> It was taught, R. Jose son of R. Judah said: Two ministering angels accompany man on the eve of the Sabbath from the synagogue to his home, one a good [angel] and one an evil [one]. And when he arrives home and finds the lamp burning, the table laid and the couch [bed] covered with a spread, the good angel exclaims, ''May it be even thus on another Sabbath,'' and the evil angel unwillingly answers ''amen.'' But if not, the evil angel exclaims, ''May it be even thus on another Sabbath,'' and the good angel unwillingly responds ''Amen.'' (Talmud *Shabbat* 119b)

Occasionally angels will be used by the Rabbis in the Midrash as accusers of the Israelites for some offense that they have committed. In the following example, the angels of God accuse the Israelites of being idolatrous:

> When the Israelites went into exile, the angels of the service said to God, ''When Israel was in her land, she was addicted to idolatry. Now that You have exiled them among the Gentiles, surely they will serve idols all the more.'' God answered the

angels, "I trust my sons that they will not abandon Me and cleave to idols. They will give their lives for My sake every hour. . . ." (*Pesikta Rabbati,* 160a)

Finally, angels were often perceived by the Rabbis as having the ability to stop a person's prayer from reaching God. In this example, the angels attempt to interfere with the prayer of the very wicked King Manasseh:

In distress King Manasseh called on God, and said, "I have called on all of the gods of the world, and I realize that there is no reality in them. You are God over all the gods, but if you do not answer me, I may think that all the gods, including You, are equal." God said to him, "You wicked one, you deserve that I should not answer you, for you have provoked Me to anger, but so as not to shut the door upon the repentant, lest they should say, 'Manasseh sought to repent, but was not received,' therefore I will answer you." The angels of the service stopped up the windows of the firmament, so that Manasseh's prayer should not ascend to heaven, but God broke through the firmament under the throne of His glory, and received his prayer. (*Deuteronomy Rabbah, Va'etchanan,* 2, 20)

GOD IS A CREATOR, AND THE DIRECTING AND SUPERVISING FORCE OF THE UNIVERSE

The Rabbis held the belief that God was the single power in the Universe that determined and directed it in accordance with a preordained plan and in conformity with a definite purpose. In order to concretize this belief, the Rabbis often utilized legendary parables. They were particularly fond of the parable of the ship and the captain or the parable of the building and its owner:

Rabbi Jochanan and Resh Lakish discussed this. Rabbi Jochanan said: When a mortal king builds a palace, after having built the lower stories, he builds the upper ones; but the Holy One blessed be He, created the upper stories and the lower stories in a single act. Rabbi Simeon ben Lakish said: When a human being builds a ship, first he brings the beams, then the ropes. After this he procures the anchors, and then erects the masts. But the Holy One, blessed be He, created them [heaven and earth] and their crew, as it is written, Thus says God, He that created the heavens and stretched them forth—"venotechem" [Isaiah 42:5]; this is written "venawtechem" (and their mariners).

GOD'S AWESOMENESS DEFIES
HUMAN COMPREHENSION

Some parables found in rabbinic texts were intended to bring about reverence for the might of God. Here is an example from the talmudic tractate of *Chullin,* 59b:

Rabbi Joshua be Chananiah traveled to Rome to speak with the Emperor on behalf of the Jews.

Hadrian's rules made life difficult for Rabbi Joshua's people, especially the rules that demanded that they must pray to Roman gods.

In the past, Emperor Hadrian had always asked Rabbi Joshua difficult questions. But each time, Rabbi Joshua had an answer for him.

I wonder what he will ask me this time? thought Rabbi Joshua as he neared the palace. Walking to the palace, Rabbi Joshua noticed statues of the Roman gods. Finally, the Rabbi met face to face with the Emperor. The Emperor said, "I have a question for you."

Rabbi Joshua nodded in a humble manner, as was his custom. The Emperor stood up and waved his arm toward the statues flanking his magnificent throne. "Our gods have faces," he said. "Why doesn't yours? I want you to show me the face of your God. I want to know what your God looks like."

"It says in the Torah that no one can see God and live," replied Rabbi Joshua.

"Nonsense. Who could believe in a God he cannot even see?"

Rabbi Joshua considered the Emperor's question carefully. He knew that if he made a mistake, Hadrian might make the laws worse or even take away the Jewish people's freedom entirely. Finally, Rabbi Joshua said, "Come outside with me and I will show you my answer."

The Emperor followed Rabbi Joshua into the bright courtyard of the palace. Rabbi Joshua faced the Emperor.

"You must look up straight at the sun to discover our God," he said.

"But of course I cannot," the Emperor replied. "You know that none can look directly at the sun."

"If you cannot look at the sun's face, how do you expect to look at the face of God?" asked Rabbi Joshua. "The sun is merely a servant of God and its brilliance is infinitely small compared with the brilliance of God's presence."

The Emperor had no answer to give Rabbi Joshua and so he dismissed him. The Rabbi returned to his homeland where he and his people continued to pray to the God one cannot see.

GOD IS NEAR TO THE MASSES

If there is a difference between the biblical concept of God and that of the Talmud, it lies in the fact that the talmudic God is more "homey" so to speak, near to the masses or ordinary people in need of help. And so we find that God mourns because of the evil decrees He has pronounced upon Israel ("Before God brought on the flood, God Himself kept seven days of mourning, for He grieved at heart" [Genesis 6: 6 *Tanchuma, Shemini* 11a].) and goes into exile with His children when they go into exile. ("Come and see how beloved of God are the children of Israel, for wherever they were exiled, God went into exile with them" [Talmud *Megillah* 29a].) When the Israelites study the Law, God or His Shechinah is also among them: "Rabbi Chanina ben Teradion said: If two sit together and words of Torah are between them, the Shechinah rests between them, and if even one sits and occupies himself with Torah, God fixes for him a reward" (*Ethics of the Fathers,* 3, 3).

The concept of God's nearness to man is also enshrined in one of the rabbinic ethical teachings. The Rabbis commanded man to imitate the attributes of God: "Just as God is merciful and compassionate, you also should be merciful and compassionate" (*Mechilta BeShallach* 14:2).

In a second example, we are told by the Rabbis that "just as God clothes the naked, visits the sick, comforts the mourners and buries the dead, so should you as well" (Talmud *Soṭah* 14a).

GOD AND THE ISRAELITES
ARE LOVING PARTNERS

The Rabbis continued to expand upon the concept of the special bond between the Jewish people and God that had been established during biblical times. The love relationship between Israel and the Jewish people is an eternal one, and can never be broken. Here are several examples of the special bond of love between God and the Israelites: "Even if all of the idolaters were to gather to quench the love between God and Israel, they would be powerless" (*Exodus Rabbah, Vayakhel* 49:1). "Hillel said in the name of God by way of illustration of the covenant of love between God and Israel: 'My feet carry Me to the place which My heart loves. If you come to My house I will come to yours; but if you do not come to My house I will not come to yours' " (*Tosefta Sukkah,* 4, 3).

GOD AND SUFFERING OF GOOD PEOPLE

The Rabbis were challenged by the fact that righteous people often seem to suffer while so-called evil people prosper. They did not deal in great length with the problem of theodicy (i.e., why there is evil in the world), but rather spent most of their writings discussing the response that a person should have to his or her own suffering.

At times the Rabbis assumed that suffering was a result of one's sins and transgressions: "Rabba says, 'If a person sees that painful suffering comes to him, let him examine his conduct.' For it is said: 'Let us search and try our ways, and return unto God' (Lamentations 3:40). If he examines and finds nothing objectionable, let him attribute it to the neglect of the study of the Torah. For it is written: 'Happy is the man whom You chasten, O God, and teach out of Your Law' (Psalm 94:12). If he did attribute it thus, and still did not find this to be the cause, let him be sure that these are chastenings of love. For it is said: 'For whom the Lord loves he corrects' (Proverbs 3:12)."

In the following example, we learn that the Rabbis hoped that one would accept his sufferings, due to the fact that suffering often leads to world salvation:

Rabbi Joshua ben Levi said: "He who gladly accepts the sufferings of this world brings salvation to the world" (Talmud *Taanit* 8a).

We are also told by the Rabbis that suffering can atone for one's sins: "Beloved are sufferings, for they appease like offerings. They are more beloved than offerings, for guilt and sin offerings atone only for the particular sin for which they are brought in each case, but sufferings atone for **all** sins" (*Midrash Psalms* 118:18).

Midrashim on the Exodus story have depicted God as suffering with the Israelites in their struggle for redemption: "The Redemption is for Me and for you. It is as if I will be redeemed with you, as it says 'the nations and their gods' " (*Exodus Rabbah* 15:12).

Pain and suffering were also viewed as a by-product of progress. Pain, the Rabbis stated, was essential to some desirable end. It helps to fulfill some providential purpose and is subservient to some benign purpose. Pain is a by-product of birth. Thus, the Rabbis in a sense viewed suffering and pain as a necessary concomitant of progress and growth. As one rabbinic sage put it, "Pain and suffering should lead to liberty" (Talmud *Berakhot* 5a); and another, "If you want life, expect pain" (*Midrash Psalms* 16:11).

Finally, in the *Ethics of the Fathers* (4:19), we find the adage "It is not in our power to explain either the prosperity of the wicked or the afflictions of the righteous." The Rabbis adopted the conclusion of the biblical Book of Job, "Who can understand the thunder of God's mighty deeds?" Ultimately, to understand why people suffer may be totally beyond the comprehension of humankind.

NEW RABBINIC NAMES FOR GOD

The subject of the names of God in rabbinic literature can be divided into two headings: the prohibition of using the biblical Divine Names and the additional names evolved by the Rabbis.

The prohibition of using biblical Divine Names applied both to the pronunciation of the name of God and its committal to writing. The prohibition against the pronunciation of God's name applied only to the four letter name of God—*Adonai* (called the Tetragrammaton), which could be pronounced only by the High Priest on the Day of Atonement in the Holy of Holies and in the Jerusalem Temple by the priests when they recited the Priestly Blessing. The Rabbis also forbade the erasing of God's seven biblical names (i.e., *El, Elohim,* "I am that I am," *Adonai, Shaddai, Tzevaot,* and YHVH) from a written document.

The Rabbis also evolved a number of new names for God, all references to God's many attributes and characteristics. They include the following: The Great, The Majestic, *Hakadosh Baruch Hu* (Holy One Blessed be He), *Ribbono shel Olam* (Sovereign of the Universe), *Hamakom* (The Place), *HaRachaman* (The All Merciful One), *Avinu Shebashamayim* (Our Father in Heaven), *Ani* (I), *Shalom* (Peace), *Temira detemirin* (Hidden of Hiddens), *Attika deattikin* (Ancient of Ancients), *Ein Sof* (Without End).

Each of these names manifests a different part of God's essence. For example: "Rabbi Huna in the name of Rabbi Ammi said, 'Why do we use a circumlocution for the name of the Holy One, blessed be He, and call him **Makom**? Because He is the place of His world, but this world is not His [only] place' " (*Genesis Rabbah* 68:49).

In this final example, we clearly see that the Rabbis believed that each different name for God did not represent a different god, but rather a different manifestation of one of God's many attributes:

Rabbi Abba ben Mammel said: God said to Moses: "You wish to know My name. Well, I am called according to My work. Sometimes I am called 'Almighty God,' 'Lord of Hosts,' 'Lord.' When I am judging created beings, I am called 'God,' and when I am waging war against the wicked, I am called 'Lord of Hosts.' When I suspend judgment for a person's sins, I am called 'El Shaddai' (Almighty God), and when I am merciful towards My world, I am called 'Adonai,' for 'Adonai' refers to the Attribute of Mercy, as it is said: 'The Lord, the Lord' (Adonai, Adonai), God, merciful and gracious. . . ." (*Exodus Rabbah* 3:6)

SUMMARY

The rabbinic view of God enhances that of the biblical view by adding imagery, parable, allegory, and legend. Although there is no systemized rabbinic theology, there are a number of consistent teachings that are part of the broad consensus on what God meant to the Rabbis of many centuries ago:

1. God is a One and Only God.
2. God is omnipresent.
3. God created and directs the universe.
4. God has facilitators who take the form of angels.
5. God's omnipotence is beyond all human comprehension.
6. God is near to those who call upon Him.

7. No one can ever truly understand human suffering.
8. God has a special loving relationship with the Jewish people.
9. God has many different attributes and names.

7

GOD IN JEWISH MYSTICISM

Jewish mystics, known in Hebrew as kabbalists, think very deeply about how a person could and should imagine God. Their approach is that man cannot know what God is, but man can understand the powers that God used to create and sustain the universe, and govern the people in it.

In terms of God Himself, God has, in mystical thought, neither a name nor an attribute, and nothing can be said of Him except that He is. This absolute divinity is called in Jewish mysticism *Ein Sof* (the Infinite). And God's mysterious powers are known as *sefirot* (emanations of God).

The word *Ein Sof* means infinite and without end. For the kabbalists, God is not limited by space, has no physical form, and God's being extends without end. God is everywhere, and God is greater than the entire universe. God is also eternal and thus can never be limited to time. Because God is infinite, what God really is cannot be imagined by humankind. Since that which God really is must always remain a mystery, the mystics speak of this aspect of God as "the hidden God."

As to the question of how the kabbalists conceive of God creating the world and man, the kabbalists discovered *sefirot,* divine luminaries or spheres through which God is revealed. The word *sefirot* comes from the Hebrew word *sappir* (sapphire), because the mystics compare the brightness of God to that of a sapphire stone. They think of the *sefirot* as spheres of very bright light sent forth by God when He created the world. Through these *sefirot,* say the kabbalists, the world came into being and is preserved. There were ten *sefirot* that God used in creating the world. Their names are *keter* (crown), *chochmah* (wisdom), *binah* (understanding), *chesed* (mercy), *din* or *gevurah* (judgment or power), *tiferet* (beauty), *netzach* (eternity), *hod* (majesty), *yesod* (foundation), and *malchut* (kingdom).

The ten *sefirot* form a hierarchy: *keter,* the highest of the *sefirot,* is considered to be the closest to the *Ein Sof. Keter* is the name for the will of God. Thus, when God began to create the world, His first step was to exert His will to create. Similarly, after God willed the creation of the world, He thought about all of the possible ways to bring the world into existence. Thus, the name for God's thought or wisdom was the second *sefirah—chochmah* (wisdom).

Next, God decided on a specific plan that would be the best choice of action for creating the world. The name for God's understanding was the third *sefirah— binah.*

To visualize the balance between *chochmah* and *bina* in God, Jewish mystics see these two *sefirot* flowing from *keter* in this way:

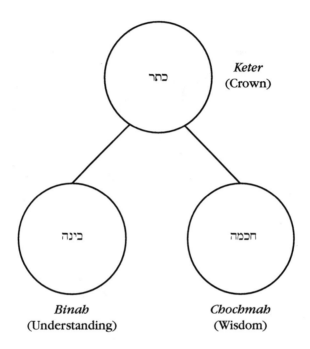

Keter
(Crown)

Binah
(Understanding)

Chochmah
(Wisdom)

These first three *sefirot* stand for the powers of God's mind, which God used to plan the creation of the world.

Now God needed several additional principles with which to govern the world that He created. The fourth *sefirah, chesed,* God's mercy or kindness, was balanced by *din* (judgment), the fifth *sefirah.* To create the necessary harmony between these two *sefirot* of mercy and judgment, a sixth *sefirah* was necessary, called *tiferet* (beauty). The mystics visualized these middle three *sefirot* in this way:

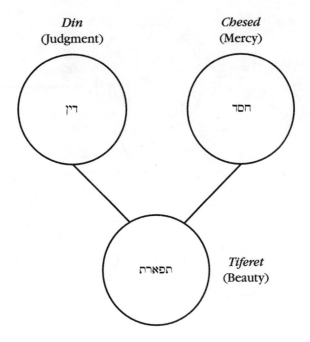

The middle three *sefirot* stand for the moral principles that God uses to rule the world.

It became apparent to the mystics that the *sefirot* of mercy and judgment are not always balanced. When the sins of people exceed their good deeds, *din* (God's judgment) is no longer balanced with *chesed* (kindness). This is one reason that evil comes into the world. But when the good deeds outweigh the sins of people, there is harmony in heaven, represented by *tiferet*.

The third group of *sefirot* stands for God's principles of ruling the natural, physical world. The mystics believed that God's powers had both male and female aspects. The male aspect was represented on the right side of the *sefirot,* and the female on the left.

The seventh sefirah—*netzach* or eternity—stands for the male aspect of God's powers. It represents the power of nature to increase herself.

The eighth *sefirah—hod* (majesty) stands for the limiting aspect of nature, always keeping a check on the *sefirah* of *netzach.*

The ninth *sefirah,* balancing *netzach* and *hod,* represents the harmony of nature. It is called *yesod* (foundation), and represents the balance of nature. These three *sefirot* can be visualized in this way:

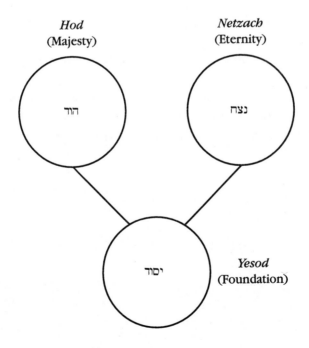

Hod
(Majesty)

Netzach
(Eternity)

הוד

נצח

יסוד

Yesod
(Foundation)

The kabbalists believe that God's love for the Jewish people was so great that He wished to reveal His presence to them. Often comparing God's love for Israel to the love of a king for a queen, the tenth and final *sefirah—malchut—*represents the union of God, the King, with His queen (the people of Israel). This *sefirah* is also known as the *Shechinah—*God's presence. The union of God with Israel is the climax of creation.

Here, then, is a visualization of all of the *sefirot* together:

The mystics believe that by meditating on the *sefirot* that they are connecting themselves with God's creative powers and God's actual Presence as it "poured forth" in creation. Human beings are a microcosm of the universe, and unite the "upper" and "lower" worlds. Traces of God, embodied in the *sefirot,* are found in everything and discernible in everything—at least to the mystic who knows how to interpret the symbolic language of outer reality. For mystics, God not only revealed Himself at Mount Sinai, but in everything since the beginning of the creation. God will continue to reveal Himself until the end of time.

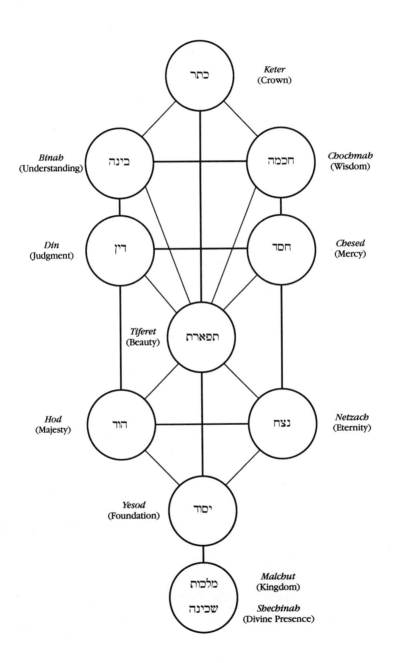

Keter
(Crown)

Binah
(Understanding)

Chochmah
(Wisdom)

Din
(Judgment)

Chesed
(Mercy)

Tiferet
(Beauty)

Hod
(Majesty)

Netzach
(Eternity)

Yesod
(Foundation)

Malchut
(Kingdom)

Shechinah
(Divine Presence)

8

GOD TALK, PRAYER, AND THE PRAYER BOOK

Prayer is the natural expression of the religious feelings of people. In the Jewish tradition, prayer occupies a central position. From the dawn of human history, the sacrificial offering was the basis of Divine worship. It was not until Abraham made his covenant with God that there arose a people who broke away from idol worship and turned to worship of One God. The Bible records numerous instances of prayer, many of which were spontaneous. When "Abraham prayed to God" (Genesis 20:17) and when he pleaded with God on behalf of the people of Sodom (Genesis 18:23), he set precedents followed by his descendants after him.

Eventually the Temple at Jerusalem became the major place of prayer. Those who could not be there physically at least turned to it when worshiping. In the Temple, the Levites sang and probably composed many of the Psalms. The most famous prayer of all, the *Shema Yisrael,* and the Ten Commandments were recited daily.

When the first Temple was destroyed in 586 B.C.E. and the Jews were exiled to Babylon, lacking a central house of worship, they began to assemble on a regular basis to talk, pray, and study. Thus, according to one theory, the synagogue was born.

By the early days of the second Temple (400 B.C.E.), some form of group prayer existed. As more and more synagogues emerged, especially by the time of the Middle Ages (800 C.E.), prayer services followed. By the ninth century C.E., the Jewish scholars in Spain appealed to Rav Amram, the head of the Sura academy in Babylon, to supply them with a guide to the correct order of the prayers. It was in response to this request that Rav Amram produced the first complete written prayer book. Another head of the Academy in Sura, Saadia Gaon, created another prayer book. Many new liturgical poems were included in his prayer book. These two prayer books, those of Amram and Saadia, have given to the traditional prayer book its basic structure as we know it today.

PRAYER IN RABBINIC THOUGHT

On the biblical verse "and serve him with all your heart" (Deuteronomy 11:13), the Rabbis commented: "What is service of the heart? It is prayer." Perhaps the best-known mystical statement on prayer is the comment in the *Zohar,* the Book of Mysticism, on the wondrous ladder of Jacob's dream, whose "feet stood on earth and whose head reached to the very heavens" (Genesis 28:12). "This ladder," says the *Zohar,* is prayer.

For the Jew today, prayer is a way of relating to himself, to his fellow person, and to God. Worshipers turn to prayer for a variety of different reasons— strength, comfort, fellowship, self-expression, self-assessment, and identity. It is through the prayers of the prayer book that we can learn about how their writers conceived and "pictured" God. The following are examples of prayers from the prayer book. Each prayer will be followed with several remarks related to the occasion for which the prayer is to be chanted and what we can learn about the way in which God is portrayed.

1. *Modeh Ani:* I thank you, living and enduring King, for restoring my soul to me in compassion. You are faithful beyond measure.

This prayer is traditionally recited immediately upon arising in the morning. In it, God is called the enduring King. One expresses gratitude for daily renewal of both physical and mental strength.

2. *Asher Yatzar:* Praised are You, Lord our God, King of the Universe, who with wisdom fashioned the human body, creating openings, arteries, glands and organs. . . . Should one of them be blocked, it would be impossible to exist. Praised are You, Lord, Healer of all flesh who sustains our bodies in wondrous ways.

This prayer is traditionally recited after going to the bathroom. It praises God for the wonders of the body, and implies that people ought not take for granted even the routine act of eliminating wastes. In this prayer God is called the *Rofeh*—the Healer. This prayer has led to the creation of other prayers for the ill, in which God is petitioned to use His powers of healing to cure the ill.

3. *The blessing said upon visiting a place where one experienced a miraculous rescue:* Praised are You, Lord our God, King of the Universe, who granted me a miracle in this place.

This blessing is recited upon visiting a place where one experienced a miraculous rescue. It is an indication that the Rabbis not only believed that God could assist in a person's rescue, but that proper gratitude to God was necessary when such a rescue occurred.

4. *Avinu Malkenu:* Our Father, our King, we have sinned before You, Our Father, our king, we have no King but You . . .

This prayer is recited between the festivals of Rosh Hashanah (the Jewish New Year), Yom Kippur (the Day of Atonement), and on fast days. In this prayer God is called both a Father and a King. Thus, the Rabbis conceived of God as both immanent and transcendent, and that people can and should relate to God intimately as a child to a father with warmth and openness and as a King, Ruler, awesome, distant, and unknowable. This prayer petitions God for the fulfillment of a variety of requests (including the annulment of evil decrees and forgiveness for sins).

5. *Emet V'Emunah:* We affirm the truth that He is our God, that there is no other, and that we are His people Israel. He redeems us from the power of kings, delivers us from the hand of all tyrants. He brings judgment upon our oppressors, retribution upon all our mortal enemies. He performs wonders beyond understanding, marvels beyond reckoning. He has maintained us among the living. He has not allowed our steps to falter. He guided us to triumph over mighty foes, exalted our strength over all our enemies. He vindicated us with miracles before Pharaoh.

This prayer affirms a number of basic rabbinic concepts related to God and God's attributes. Among these attributes are God's Unity, God the Redeemer, God of justice, God the Guider of humankind, and God whose awesome powers are beyond all human understanding.

6. *Ahavat Olam:* With constancy You have loved your people Israel, teaching us Torah and *mitzvot,* statutes and laws. Therefore, Lord our God, when we lie down to sleep and when we rise, we shall think of Your laws and speak of them, rejoicing in Your Torah and *mitzvot* always. For they are our life and the length of our days. We will meditate on them day and night. Never take away Your love from us. Praised are You, Lord, who loves His people Israel.

In this prayer, *Ahavat Olam* (with everlasting love), we learn that God has shown His love for Israel by giving them commandments (*mitzvot*) by which to live. Jewish people are charged with the responsibility of constantly thinking and doing God's commandments and living by them. In this way they show their love and faith in God, who will with constancy love the Jewish people.

7. *Ahavah Rabbah* (With abounding love . . .): With abounding love have you loved us, O Lord our God, and great and flowing tenderness have You shown us. O our Father, our King, for our father's sake, who trusted in You, and whom You did teach the statutes of life, be gracious to us and teach us. O our Father, merciful Father, ever compassionate, have mercy upon us. Put into our hearts to understand and to discern, to mark, learn and teach, to heed, to do and to fulfill in love all the words of instruction in your Torah. Enlighten our eyes in your Torah, and let our hearts cleave to your commandments, and unify our hearts to love and revere

Your Name, so that we be never put to shame. Because we have trusted in Your holy, great, and revered Name, we shall rejoice and be glad in your saving power. O bring us peace from the four corners of the earth, and make us go upright to our land, for you are a God who works salvation. You have chosen us from all peoples and tongues, and have brought us near to Your great Name forever in faithfulness, that we might in love give thanks to you and proclaim Your unity. Blessed are You, O Lord, who has chosen Your people Israel in love.

This prayer precedes the *Shema Yisrael* prayer. It is a praise of God's goodness for giving the Israelites His teaching, and a prayer for His help in the study of the Torah. It also recalls God's constant love for the ancestors. There is a strain of passionate love of God in this prayer, which stresses the love of God and the selection of Israel, on the duty of obeying God's commandments. The prayer closes with the benediction that God has selected Israel as His chosen people.

8. *First paragraph of the Amidah:* Praised are You, Lord our God and God of our father, God of Abraham, God of Isaac, and God of Jacob, the great, mighty and revered God, the most high God, who bestows lovingkindness, and is Master of all things; who remembers the pious deeds of the patriarchs, and in love will bring a redeemer to their children's children for Your Name's sake. O King, Helper, Savior and Shield. Blessed are You, O Lord, Shield of Abraham.

In this prayer (the opening blessing of the *Amidah*, literally the "standing prayer," because it is recited while standing) one proclaims that God is the God of the Israelite patriarchs and was their protector as He is the protector of the Jewish people. The prayer appeals to the "merit" of the patriarchs as a way of urging God to care for us.

9. *Aleynu:* We rise to our duty to praise the Lord of all, to acclaim the Creator. He made our lot unlike that of other people, assigning to us a unique destiny. We bend the knee and bow, acknowledging the King of kings, the Holy One Blessed be He, who spread out the heavens and laid the foundations of the earth, whose glorious abode is in the highest heaven, whose mighty dominion is in the loftiest heights. He is our God, there is no other. In truth, He alone is our King, as it is written in His Torah: "Know this day and take it to heart that the Lord is God in heaven above and on earth below; there is no other."

This prayer praises God for His creation of the universe and for choosing the Jewish people to work for the establishment of God's Kingdom on earth. God's Oneness and Unity are emphasized at the conclusion of the prayer.

10. *Yigdal:*

The living God we praise, exalt, adore
He was, He is, He will be evermore.

No unity like unto His can be
Eternal, inconceivable is He.

No form, or shape has the incorporeal One
Most holy He, past all comparison.

He was, ere aught was made in heaven, or earth,
But His existence has no date, or birth.

Lord of the Universe is He proclaimed
Teaching His power to all His hand has framed.

He gave His gift of prophecy to those
In whom He gloried, whom He loved and chose.

No prophet ever yet has filled the place
Of Moses, who beheld God face to face.

Through Him the faithful in His house the Lord
The law of truth to Israel did accord.

This Law God will not alter, will not change
For any other through time's utmost range.

He knows and heeds the secret thoughts of people:
He saw the end of all ere aught began.

With love and grace does He the righteous bless.
He metes out evil unto wickedness.

He at the last will His anointed send,
Those to redeem, who hope, and wait the end.

God will the dead to life again restore.
Praised be His glorious Name for evermore.

This prayer, which concludes the Friday evening liturgy, is a poetic reiteration of the Jewish creed of faith as formulated by the eleventh-century philosopher Moses Maimonides. Each of his so-called Thirteen Principles of Faith begins with the formula "I believe that . . ." The articles that relate to God in this prayer can be summarized as follows:

1. the belief in the existence of a Creator.
2. the belief in God's unity.

3. God has no form.
4. God is eternal.
5. All worship and adoration are due God alone.
6. All of the words of the Prophets are true.
7. Moses was the greatest Prophet.
8. God revealed His Torah at Mount Sinai.
9. God's Torah is immutable.
10. God knows the actions of people.
11. God rewards and punishes in justice.
12. God will bring a Messiah.
13. God will resurrect the dead.

11. *Adon Olam* (Eternal God)

The Lord eternal reigned before the birth of every living thing.

When all was made as He ordained, then only He was known as King.

When all is ended He will reign alone in awesome majesty.

He was, He is, and He will be, glorious in eternity.

Peerless and unique is He, with none at all to be compared.

Beginningless and endless, His vast dominion is not shared.

He is my God, my life's redeemer, my refuge in distress,

My shelter sure, my cup of life, His goodness limitless.

I place my spirit in His care, when I wake as when I sleep.

God is with me, I shall not fear, body and spirit
in His keep.

This concluding prayer presents a dual conception of
God: God's distance from people (Lord of the world,
who was King before existence was created) and God's
closeness (My God, my Redeemer, my Refuge, my Shelter). The prayer stresses God's unity and eternity. Finally, one is reminded that one can always trust God
who is available to people any day and every day. And as
the years multiply and people approach the end of their
days, belief in God can help them to calmly surrender
their bodies.

BLESSINGS FOR GOD

The basic building block of all Jewish prayer is the blessing, known in Hebrew as *beracha*. All blessings include the six-word Hebrew formula *Barukh ata Adonai
eloheinu melekh ha'olam*—Blessed are You, Adonai our
God, Sovereign of the Universe. Rabbinic authorities have
recommended that one hundred blessings a day are easily
recited by a person who follows the regimen of prayer.
Each small acceptance helps weave the attitude of gratitude into the texture of everyday existence, so that it can
ultimately penetrate the deeper levels of consciousness.

Blessings serve a variety of purposes. They can be used
to thank God for the many blessings people have received
from God's hand. When one thanks God for a gift received, one also assumes an ethical responsibility for that
gift. For example, when a person says a blessing thanking

God for food, the ethical implication is that one who is grateful for food will be involved in caring for the earth.

A third aspect of the blessing involves appreciation of the world—its beauty and wonders. (e.g., a beautiful sunset, rainbow, and so forth) Finally, saying a blessing to God provides a person with an opportunity to reach out beyond oneself and to connect to God.

Here is a summary of some of the major blessings for which one can bless God. One can see from this range of blessings all of the gifts that the Rabbis believed God has bestowed upon people. In addition, it becomes readily apparent that blessings to God need not be confined to the synagogue or limited to the formal religious service.

BLESSINGS FOR TASTE

Bread

בָּרוּךְ אַתָּה יהוה אֱלֹהֵינוּ מֶלֶךְ הָעוֹלָם, הַמּוֹצִיא לֶחֶם מִן הָאָרֶץ.

Blessed are You, *Adonai* Our God, Sovereign of the Universe, who brings forth bread from the earth.

Barukh atah Adonai eloheinu melekh ha'olam hamotzi lechem min baaretz.

Food (other than bread) prepared from wheat, barley, rye, oats, or spelt:

בָּרוּךְ אַתָּה יהוה אֱלֹהֵינוּ מֶלֶךְ הָעוֹלָם, בּוֹרֵא מִינֵי מְזוֹנוֹת.

Blessed are You, *Adonai* Our God, Sovereign of the Universe, who creates different kinds of nourishment.

Barukh atah Adonai eloheinu melekh ha'olam borei meenei mezonote.

Wine

בָּרוּךְ אַתָּה יהוה אֱלֹהֵינוּ מֶלֶךְ הָעוֹלָם, בּוֹרֵא פְּרִי הַגָּפֶן.

Blessed are You, *Adonai* Our God, Sovereign of the Universe, who creates the fruit of the vine.
Barukh atah Adonai eloheinu melekh ha'olam borei pri hagafen.

Fruit

בָּרוּךְ אַתָּה יהוה אֱלֹהֵינוּ מֶלֶךְ הָעוֹלָם, בּוֹרֵא פְּרִי הָעֵץ.

Blessed are You, *Adonai* Our God; Sovereign of the Universe, who creates the fruit of the tree.
Barukh atah Adonai eloheinu melekh ha'olam borei pri ha'eitz.

Foods that grow in the ground

בָּרוּךְ אַתָּה יהוה אֱלֹהֵינוּ מֶלֶךְ הָעוֹלָם, בּוֹרֵא פְּרִי הָאֲדָמָה.

Blessed are You, *Adonai,* Our God, Sovereign of the Universe, who creates the fruit of the ground.
Barukh atah Adonai eloheinu melekh ha'olam borei pri haadamah.

Other food and drink

בָּרוּךְ אַתָּה יהוה אֱלֹהֵינוּ מֶלֶךְ הָעוֹלָם, שֶׁהַכֹּל נִהְיֶה בִּדְבָרוֹ.

Blessed are You, *Adonai* Our God, Sovereign of the Universe, at whose word all things come into existence.
Barukh atah Adonai eloheinu melekh ha'olam shehakol nihiyeh bidvaro.

BLESSINGS FOR SMELL

Upon smelling fragrant spices

בָּרוּךְ אַתָּה יהוה אֱלֹהֵינוּ מֶלֶךְ הָעוֹלָם, בּוֹרֵא מִינֵי בְשָׂמִים.

Blessed are You, *Adonai* Our God, Sovereign of the Universe, who creates different kinds of spices.
Barukh atah Adonai eloheinu melekh ha'olam borei mine vesamim.

Upon smelling the fragrance of shrubs and trees

בָּרוּךְ אַתָּה יהוה אֱלֹהֵינוּ מֶלֶךְ הָעוֹלָם, בּוֹרֵא עֲצֵי בְשָׂמִים.

Blessed are You, *Adonai* Our God, Sovereign of the Universe, who creates fragrant trees.
Barukh atah Adonai eloheinu melekh ha'olam borei atzei vesamim.

Upon smelling the fragrance of plants and herbs

בָּרוּךְ אַתָּה יהוה אֱלֹהֵינוּ מֶלֶךְ הָעוֹלָם, בּוֹרֵא עִשְׂבֵי בְשָׂמִים.

Blessed are You, *Adonai* Our God, Sovereign of the Universe, who creates fragrant plants.
Barukh atah Adonai eloheinu melekh ha'olam borei isvei vesamim.

Upon smelling fragrant fruit

בָּרוּךְ אַתָּה יהוה אֱלֹהֵינוּ מֶלֶךְ הָעוֹלָם, הַנּוֹתֵן רֵיחַ טוֹב בַּפֵּרוֹת.

Blessed are You, *Adonai* Our God, Sovereign of the Universe, who gives a pleasant fragrance to fruits.
Barukh atah Adonai eloheinu melekh ha'olam hanotein rei'ach tov bapeirot.

Upon smelling fragrant oils

בָּרוּךְ אַתָּה יהוה אֱלֹהֵינוּ מֶלֶךְ הָעוֹלָם, בּוֹרֵא שֶׁמֶן עָרֵב.

Blessed are You, *Adonai* Our God, Sovereign of the Universe, who creates fragrant oil.

Barukh atah Adonai eloheinu melekh ha'olam borei shemen areiv.

BLESSINGS FOR SIGHT

Upon seeing a rainbow

בָּרוּךְ אַתָּה יהוה אֱלֹהֵינוּ מֶלֶךְ הָעוֹלָם, זוֹכֵר הַבְּרִית וְנֶאֱמָן בִּבְרִיתוֹ וְקַיָם בְּמַאֲמָרוֹ.

Blessed are You, *Adonai* Our God, Sovereign of the Universe, who remembers the covenant and is faithful to all promises.

Barukh atah Adonai eloheinu melekh ha'olam zokher haberit vene'eman bivrito vekayam bemaamaro.

Upon seeing trees blossoming
for the first time in the year

בָּרוּךְ אַתָּה יהוה אֱלֹהֵינוּ מֶלֶךְ הָעוֹלָם, שֶׁלֹּא חִסַּר בְּעוֹלָמוֹ דָּבָר, וּבָרָא בוֹ בְּרִיוֹת טוֹבוֹת וְאִילָנוֹת טוֹבִים לְהַנוֹת בָּהֶם בְּנֵי אָדָם.

Blessed are You, *Adonai* Our God, Sovereign of the Universe, who has withheld nothing from the world and who has created lovely creatures and beautiful trees for people to enjoy.

Barukh atah Adonai eloheinu melekh ha'olam shelo chisar be'olamo davar uvara vo briyot tovot ve'ilanot tovim lehanot bahem benei adam.

Upon seeing the ocean

בָּרוּךְ אַתָּה יהוה אֱלֹהֵינוּ מֶלֶךְ הָעוֹלָם, שֶׁעָשָׂה אֶת־הַיָּם הַגָּדוֹל.

Blessed are You, *Adonai* Our God, Sovereign of the Universe, who has made the great sea.
Barukh atah Adonai eloheinu melekh ha'olam she'asah et hayam hagadol.

Upon seeing trees or creatures of unusual beauty

בָּרוּךְ אַתָּה יהוה אֱלֹהֵינוּ מֶלֶךְ הָעוֹלָם, שֶׁכָּכָה לּוֹ בְּעוֹלָמוֹ.

Blessed are You, *Adonai* Our God, Sovereign of the Universe, who has such beauty in the world.
Barukh atah Adonai eloheinu melekh ha'olam shekakhah lo be'olamo.

Upon seeing someone of abnormal appearance

בָּרוּךְ אַתָּה יהוה אֱלֹהֵינוּ מֶלֶךְ הָעוֹלָם, מְשַׁנֶּה הַבְּרִיּוֹת.

Blessed are You, *Adonai* Our God, Sovereign of the Universe, who makes people different.
Barukh atah Adonai eloheinu melekh ha'olam meshaneh habriyot.

Upon seeing lightning, shooting stars, mountains, or a sunrise

בָּרוּךְ אַתָּה יהוה אֱלֹהֵינוּ מֶלֶךְ הָעוֹלָם, עֹשֶׂה מַעֲשֵׂה בְרֵאשִׁית.

Blessed are You, *Adonai* Our God, Sovereign of the Universe, Source of creation.
Barukh atah Adonai eloheinu melekh ha'olam oseh maaseh vereshit.

Upon seeing synagogues restored

בָּרוּךְ אַתָּה יהוה אֱלֹהֵינוּ מֶלֶךְ הָעוֹלָם, מַצִּיב גְּבוּל אַלְמָנָה.

Blessed are You, *Adonai* Our God, Sovereign of the Universe, who restores the borders of the widow. (Zion)
Barukh atah Adonai eloheinu melekh ha'olam matziv gevul almanah.

Upon seeing a person distinguished in knowledge of Torah

בָּרוּךְ אַתָּה יהוה אֱלֹהֵינוּ מֶלֶךְ הָעוֹלָם, שֶׁחָלַק מֵחָכְמָתוֹ לִירֵאָיו.

Blessed are You, *Adonai* Our God, Sovereign of the Universe, who has given wisdom to those who revere God.
Barukh atah Adonai eloheinu melekh ha'olam shechalak meichokhmato lirei'av.

Upon seeing a person distinguished in secular knowledge

בָּרוּךְ אַתָּה יהוה אֱלֹהֵינוּ מֶלֶךְ הָעוֹלָם, שֶׁנָּתַן מֵחָכְמָתוֹ לְבָשָׂר וָדָם.

Blessed are You, *Adonai* Our God, Sovereign of the Universe, who has given wisdom to mortals.
Barukh atah Adonai eloheinu melekh ha'olam shenatan mechokhmato levasar vadam.

Upon seeing a head of state

בָּרוּךְ אַתָּה יהוה אֱלֹהֵינוּ מֶלֶךְ הָעוֹלָם, שֶׁנָּתַן מִכְּבוֹדוֹ לְבָשָׂר וָדָם.

Blessed are You, *Adonai* Our God, Sovereign of the Universe, who has given glory to mortals.
Barukh atah Adonai eloheinu melekh ha'olam shenatan' mikvodo levasar vadam.

Upon seeing a friend after a long separation

בָּרוּךְ אַתָּה יהוה אֱלֹהֵינוּ מֶלֶךְ הָעוֹלָם, מְחַיֵּה הַמֵּתִים.

Blessed are You, *Adonai* Our God, Sovereign of the Universe, who brings the dead back to life.

Barukh atah Adonai eloheinu melekh ha'olam mechayeh hameiteem.

BLESSINGS UPON HEARING

Upon hearing thunder

בָּרוּךְ אַתָּה יהוה אֱלֹהֵינוּ מֶלֶךְ הָעוֹלָם, שֶׁכֹּחוֹ וּגְבוּרָתוֹ מָלֵא עוֹלָם.

Blessed are You, *Adonai* Our God, Sovereign of the Universe, whose might and power fill the entire world.

Barukh atah Adonai eloheinu melekh ha'olam shekocho ugevarato malei olam.

Upon hearing good news

בָּרוּךְ אַתָּה יהוה אֱלֹהֵינוּ מֶלֶךְ הָעוֹלָם, הַטּוֹב וְהַמֵּטִיב.

Blessed are You, *Adonai* Our God, Sovereign of the Universe, who is good and causes good things.

Barukh atah Adonai eloheinu melekh ha'olam hatov vehametiv.

Upon hearing tragic news

בָּרוּךְ אַתָּה יהוה אֱלֹהֵינוּ מֶלֶךְ הָעוֹלָם, דַּיַּן הָאֱמֶת.

Blessed are You, *Adonai* Our God, Sovereign of the Universe, who is the true Judge.

Barukh atah Adonai eloheinu melekh ha'olam dayan ha'emet.

OTHER BLESSINGS OF GRATITUDE

After leaving the bathroom

בָּרוּךְ אַתָּה יהוה אֱלֹהֵינוּ מֶלֶךְ הָעוֹלָם, אֲשֶׁר יָצַר אֶת הָאָדָם בְּחָכְמָה וּבָרָא בּוֹ
נְקָבִים נְקָבִים חֲלוּלִים חֲלוּלִים. גָּלוּי וְיָדוּעַ לִפְנֵי כִסֵּא כְבוֹדְךָ שֶׁאִם יִפָּתֵחַ אֶחָד
מֵהֶם אוֹ יִסָּתֵם אֶחָד מֵהֶם אִי אֶפְשָׁר לְהִתְקַיֵּם וְלַעֲמוֹד לְפָנֶיךָ. בָּרוּךְ אַתָּה יהוה
רוֹפֵא כָל בָּשָׂר וּמַפְלִיא לַעֲשׂוֹת.

Blessed are You, *Adonai* Our God, Sovereign of the
Universe, who has formed people in wisdom and created in them many orifices and hollow tubes. It is
well known that if one of them be obstructed or
broken, it would be impossible to stay alive. Blessed
are You, Healer of all flesh, who does wondrous
things.

*Barukh atah Adonai eloheinu melekh ha'olam asher
yatzar et haadam bechakhmah uvara vo nikavim
nikavim chalulim chalulim galui veyadua lifnei kisei
kevodekha she'im yipate'ach echad meihem oh yisatem
echad meihem ee'efshar lehitkayem velaamod lifa-
nekha. Barukh atah Adonai rofei kol basar umaflee
laasot.*

Upon affixing a *mezuzah* to the doorpost

בָּרוּךְ אַתָּה יהוה אֱלֹהֵינוּ מֶלֶךְ הָעוֹלָם, אֲשֶׁר קִדְּשָׁנוּ בְּמִצְוֹתָיו וְצִוָּנוּ לִקְבֹּעַ מְזוּזָה.

Blessed are You, *Adonai* Our God, Sovereign of the
Universe, who has made us distinct with commandments and commanded us to attach the *mezuzah*.

*Barukh atah Adonai eloheinu melekh ha'olam asher
kidshanu bemitzvotav vetzivanu likboah mezuzah.*

Upon obtaining a new item, tasting a new food for the first time, entering a new home, and many other new and special occasions

בָּרוּךְ אַתָּה יהוה אֱלֹהֵינוּ מֶלֶךְ הָעוֹלָם, שֶׁהֶחֱיָנוּ וְקִיְּמָנוּ וְהִגִּיעָנוּ לַזְּמַן הַזֶּה.

Blessed are You, *Adonai* Our God, Sovereign of the Universe, who has given us life, sustained us, and helped us to reach this day.

Barukh atah Adonai eloheinu melekh ha'olam shehecheyanu vikimanu vihigiyanu lazman hazeh.

GOD'S NAMES IN THE PRAYER BOOK

Since one's relationship with God often lies at the heart of prayer, the nature of one's conception of God will usually play an important role in one's willingness to participate in the prayer experience. Here is a summary of some of the names and images of God as presented in the prayer book. As you read them, you may wish to think about which names are most comfortable for you when you address God.

1. Lord
2. Adonai
3. God of Abraham
4. God of Isaac
5. God of Jacob
6. Everlasting Rock
7. Lord of Hosts
8. Holy One
9. Guardian of Israel
10. Redeemer of Israel

11. Rock of Israel
12. King
13. Creator of Heaven and Earth
14. God of Truth
15. Shield of Abraham
16. King of Kings
17. Lover of Israel
18. Father of Mercy
19. Father of the Heavens
20. Master of the Universe
21. Judge of the Earth
22. The All Good One
23. Maker of Peace
24. The Healer
25. Reviver of the Dead

SUMMARY

Many of the God concepts as presented in the liturgy are merely reiterations of those in the Bible and the rabbinic writings. The following is a summary of the major ideas of God as presented in the prayer book:

1. God is One.
2. God listens to prayer.
3. God accepts true repentance.
4. God is eternal.
5. God has no form.
6. God knows a person's innermost thoughts.
7. God loves Israel.
8. God has chosen Israel.
9. God rewards and punishes justly.

10. God can resurrect the dead.
11. God is dependable.
12. God redeems.
13. God has great power and acts in history.
14. God can bring us miracles.

9

JEWISH THEOLOGIANS AND
THEIR RESPONSES TO GOD

Important Jewish thinkers throughout the ages often had strikingly different notions about God and God's nature. This chapter will explore the theology of some of the great thinkers throughout the ages.

HELLENISTIC JEWISH PHILOSOPHY:
PHILO JUDAEUS

Jewish philosophy is said to have begun in the Diaspora community of the Hellenistic world during the second century B.C.E. and continued there until the first century C.E. It arose out of a confrontation between the Jewish religion and Greek philosophy, and had as its aim the philosophic interpretation of Judaism. Its apologetic purpose was to show that Judaism is a kind of philosophy whose conception of God is spiritual and whose ethics is rational. Jewish philosophers polemicized against the polytheism of other religions and against pagan practices.

The first Jewish philosopher appears to have been Aristobulus of Paneas (middle of the second century B.C.E.), who wrote a commentary on the Five Books of Moses, fragments of which have been preserved by Christian Church Fathers. He argued that Greek philosophers derived their teachings from the wisdom of Moses, and he interpreted the Bible allegorically. For example, he held that the expression "hand of God," which appears several times in the Five Books, refers to God's power, and ought not to be taken literally. He also maintained that wisdom (i.e., the Torah) existed prior to heaven and earth and that God's power extends through all things.

Philo Judaeus (40 c.e.) is the most important figure in Jewish Hellenism and has been credited with being the true father of what was to become the medieval philosophical tradition. He is the only Jewish Hellenistic philosopher from whom a body of works has survived. Many of these have been preserved by the Christian Church in the original Greek. The bulk of his writings deal with the Five Books of Moses and can be divided into three series of treatises.

The first series consists of an exposition of the Five Books as a legal code. The second is a philosophical interpretation of the Five Books, and the third series consists of questions and answers on the Book of Exodus.

God's Essence

In discussing God's essence, Philo maintains an extreme transcendentalism, describing God as a Unity that transcends virtue, knowledge, and even the good itself. Although God has no name and is unknowable, Philo maintains that one must strive to know God and that God is the only object worth knowing.

According to Philo, God is the "soul" of the universe, the greatest cause of everything there is. Beyond both time and place, God fills the universe.

God's Name

Philo stated that unlike rabbinic and biblical literature, it was impossible to describe God by language, and therefore, it was impossible to give God a precise name. Thus, Philo chose to refer to God as *Ontos* (Greek for "Being" or "that which exists").

Philo further holds that the only attributes that one can apply to God are the negative ones. For instance, to say that God is "just" is simply not adequate, for this description would be limiting God to a person's idea of justice. Thus, the most we can say is that God is not unjust.

Is God a Unity?

The philosophy of the Greeks influenced Philo. The Greeks held that humans were composed of the body, representing the material perishable aspect of life and that which is the foundation of evil. The soul, on the other hand, is representative of the rational mind that stands for eternal good. A problem then arises, for the Book of Genesis states (1:27) that God created man in His image. If man is composed of both a body and a soul, it would then appear that God is also separated into these two distinct parts. Philo stated that the word "image" refers to the universal Mind after which peoples' minds are created. Thus God remains a complete unity, indivisible and one.

How Can Man Relate to God?

Man is composed of body and soul, body connecting him with matter and soul with God. In order to prepare himself for God, man has to strip himself of earthly bonds (i.e., his body and senses). Philo speaks of "reaching" God. He uses the three patriarchs (Abraham, Isaac, and Jacob) as the archetypes of the three main routes to uniting with God. The three routes are called learning, nature, and training. Abraham proceeds from learning (Hagar) to virtue (Sarah), whereas Isaac as the perfect nature reaches the mystical goal without interposing an intellectual endeavor, and Jacob is rewarded for his asceticism by the fact that the "Lord" (justice) becomes to him "God," meaning that God discloses to him His higher spheres.

There is here an additional function of the doctrine of the intermediaries that present themselves to the ascending soul as so many stages on its way to God. Although the soul is not able to advance to God Himself, it may be able to reach one of God's powers. This Philo develops in an allegory of the six towns of refuge (Numbers 35), which are made to symbolize a sequence of stations on the way to God. The final goal is to reach the Divine Word.

In Jewish tradition, man is said to relate to God in ways of fear or love. Philo, like the Rabbis of old, considered fear much inferior to love. The proper attitude, he holds, is love to be directed to God.

God's Relation to the World

Even though Philo held that God is imageless and beyond the limits of human understanding, he still maintained that God cared about the world and the people who resided in it. He taught that God operates in the world through the *logos* (Greek for "speech"), which at times he identifies with the mind of God and at other times another name for God Himself. Although Philo teaches that the world is created by God, God's direct contact with the defiling quality of matter is avoided by the interposition of the *logos* or world creating power.

The teaching of the *logos* was essentially based on Philo's redesign of the fourth-century Greek philosopher's notion of forms and essences. For Plato, everything in the world was a copy of the perfect essence of that particular object or thing. Objects were perishable, but the essences and forms were eternal. Thus, for example, all of the chairs in the world have an eternal form that is independent even of God. God contemplates the essence and creates the object.

Philo did not believe that these so-called eternal forms existed outside of God. Rather, he held that these forms were not eternal but were created by God.

With regard to creation, Philo maintained that it was carried out in two successive stages, as illustrated in the biblical narrative. The first day of creation represents God's conceiving in His *logos* the world of ideas that later served as a model for the creation of the material world, represented by the other five days. In the creation of man, the only creature capable of doing evil, God needs the cooperation of subservient powers.

In Summary

Philo, borrowing freely from Plato's theory of forms, was able to balance a transcendentalist view of God with a strong immanentistic trend based on the *logos,* allowing the spiritual God to operate in the material world. For Philo, God exists, and is unknowable. It is man's challenge to develop his power of reason in order to "reach" God.

Few ancient Jewish sources mention Philo in their writings, although there are traces of Philo's influence in the Midrash. The first medieval Jewish writer to mention him is Azariah dei Rossi (*Me'or Einayim* [1886], pgs. 90–129) who Hebraicizes his name into *Yedidya*. Philo had a much greater influence on Christianity, specifically the Church Fathers. They drew on his allegorical interpretations and adopted many of his concepts, including that of the *logos*.

MEDIEVAL JEWISH PHILOSOPHY—SAADIA GAON

Medieval Jewish philosophy began in the early tenth century as part of a general cultural revival in the Islamic East, and continued in Muslim countries—North Africa, Spain, and Egypt, for some three hundred years. Saadia Gaon, an important leader of Babylonian Jewry, is often considered to be the first medieval Jewish philosopher. His major philosophic work, written in Arabic, *Kitab al-Amanar wa-al-I'tigadat,* is the earliest Jewish philosophic work from medieval times to have survived intact. It was translated into Hebrew by Judah ibn Tibbon in 1186 under the title *Sefer ha-Emunot ve-had-De'ot,* and it exercised a profound influence on Jewish thought.

Creation of the World

Saadia opens the body of his work with a discussion of creation. He maintains that the world was created in time, that its creator was other than itself, and that it was created out of nothing (i.e., *ex nihilo*). He presents four proofs for creation. In the first, invoking the principles that the world is finite in its dimension and that a finite body cannot possess an infinite force, he concludes that the force preserving the world is finite and must have a beginning and an end. In the second proof, on the basis of the fact that what is composed of two or more elements must have been put together at some point in time, he argues that the world, which is composed of many elements, must have been created at some point in time. In the third proof Saadia argues that the world is composed of various substances, all of which are the bearers of accidents. Since accidents originate in time, the world itself must have originated in time. The fourth argument is taken from the nature of time. If the world had been uncreated, time would be infinite. Infinite time cannot be traversed, and therefore, the present or any other finite moment could never have come to be. But since the present clearly exists, time cannot be infinite. Thus it follows that the world must have a beginning.

God's Nature

Saadia's concept of God's nature is based upon his view as God as the Creator. God is the cause of all corporeal existence. God is imageless and could not possibly be corporeal, for if He were, there would perforce have to be something beyond Him which was the cause of His existence. Since God is incorporeal, God cannot be subject to the corporeal qualities of quantity and number. Hence God is a unity—one.

Regarding Divine attributes, Saadia demonstrates that
an analysis of God as Creator leads to the attribution of
three essential qualities to Him: life, power, and wisdom.
Saadia states that in reality, all three of these aforemen-
tioned qualities are united in God, but people are forced
to speak of them as separate because of the limitation of
human language.

The creation of the world, Saadia states, was an act of
free will by God. God wished to benefit His creatures by
giving them the opportunity to serve Him through the
observance of *mitzvot,* commandments. Observance of
mitzvot leads to happiness (*Emunot ve'De'ot 1:4*).

God's Commandments

Saadia classifies the commandments into two categories: the rational laws (*mitzvot sichliyyot*), which have
their basis in reason, and the traditional laws (*mitzvot
shimiyyot*), ritual, and ceremonial laws, such as those
of the Jewish diet, which have no basis in reason.

All of the rational laws have these basic rational principles: First, reason deems that one express thanksgiv-
ing to one's benefactor. Thus God demands gratitude
through a person's worship of Him. Second, reason
demands that a wise person not permit himself to be
insulted. Thus it is reasonable that a wise person not
permit himself to be insulted. Hence it is reasonable that
God should prohibit man from insulting Him (i.e.,
should prohibit man from taking His name in vain).
Finally, reason demands that creatures should not harm
one another. Thus it is reasonable that God prohibit
humankind from stealing, murdering, and harming one
another in various other ways.

While the basis for observance of the traditional laws is the sole fact that they were commanded by God, Saadia states that upon careful examination, it is possible from time to time to discern the rationale for these laws. For example, the commandment to stop working on the Sabbath provides a person time to devote to spiritual concerns.

Man's Nature

Saadia holds that man is composed of a body and soul. The soul is composed of fine material and has three essential faculties: appetite, which controls growth and reproduction; spirit, which controls the emotions; and reason, which controls knowledge. A soul cannot act by itself, and thus has been placed inside of the body. By means of a person's actions and through the performance of God's commandments, a person is able to attain true happiness.

God always provides man with an opportunity to win his own reward in life. All people are given freedom of choice, and even though God may know a person's choices, God never interferes or restricts the choices that a person may take in life.

Why Do People Suffer?

Saadia was interested in the theological problem called "theodicy"—why the evil often prosper and the good suffer. His solution lies in the balance between the suffering incurred in this world and the reward in the World to Come. He suggests that righteous and good people that suffer in this world will ultimately be rewarded in the so-called World to Come.

In Summary

Saadia believed in an incorporeal single God that created the world. The creation of people by God was to enable them to serve God through performance of His commandments. By observing both the rational and irrational commandments, a person could come to attain true happiness. Saadia's many works provided his fellow Jews with spiritual guidance for years to come.

BACHYA IBN PAKUDA

This eleventh-century moral philosopher's major work was entitled *Kitab al-Hidaya ila Fradid al-Qulub,* which was written toward the end of the eleventh century. It was translated into Hebrew by Judah ibn Tibbon in 1161 under the title *Chovot Ha-Levavot* (Duties of the Heart), and in this version, it became popular and had a profound influence upon many people. The book primarily deals with how and what a Jew must observe in order to attain spiritual perfection. In the introduction to the book, Bachya divides the obligations incumbent upon the religious person as the duties of the members of the body—that is, those obligations that involve overt actions—and duties of the hearts— that is, those obligations that involve a person's inner life. The first division includes the different ritual and ethical commands in the Torah (e.g., observing the Sabbath, praying, giving charity), while the second involves beliefs (e.g., in the unity of God, trust in God, bearing a grudge, and so forth). Bachya wrote this book because he believed that the ritual and ethical observations had been overemphasized, while the duties of a person's inner life had been neglected in the writings of writers past and his own contemporaries.

Man's Duties for God

Bachya holds that God is One, and like Saadia Gaon, has given man both rational and traditional commandments to fulfill. Divine worship must always be the expression of a person's gratitude toward God. To fulfill his many duties to God, a person must practice a number of virtues. One of these is trust in God, which is based on the belief that God is good and that God has the knowledge of what is best for man. While man has, according to Bachya, the freedom of will to choose, the realization of man's actions is always dependent on God's will. Man's intentions must always coincide with his actions in aiming toward the service of God. Humility, repentance, and self-examination are essential, as are the virtues of asceticism and temperance. The observance of these virtues leads to the highest stage of the spiritual life, the love of God. True love of God is the eagerness of the soul to unite with the Divine light.

In Summary

Bachya is likely the best known of all Jewish moral philosophers. He maintains that the basis of religion is belief that God exists as a unity. He is very concerned with the inner life of the Jew, since he states that there has been an overemphasis on religious observance and the fulfillment of ritual observances. His book *Chovot Ha-Levavot* is divided into ten chapters, each of which is devoted to a particular duty of the heart. They include: the affirmation of the unity of God (*yichud*), the nature of the world disclosing the workings of God (*bechinat haolam*), Divine worship (*avodat ha-Elohim*), trust in God (*bitachon*), sincerity of purpose (*bitachon ha'ma'aseh*), humility (*keniah*), repentance (*teshuvah*), self-examination (*cheshbon hanefesh*), asceticism (*perishut*), and the love of God (*ahavat hashem*). If a person carefully observes each of these, that person is capable of attaining spiritual perfection.

Regarding a person's soul, Bachya maintains that it is celestial in origin and is placed by Divine decree within the body, where it always tends to run the risk of forgetting its mission. The human soul receives aid from the intellect and the revealed Law in achieving its goal.

Although Bachya recommends asceticism as a virtue, his interest is not a total asceticism where one entirely breaks away from society. Rather, he recommends the pursuit of the middle way, defining the genuine ascetic as one who directs all of his actions to the service of God, while at the same time fulfilling his functions in society.

The observance of all of the virtues that he discusses will lead to the love of God, and finally union or at least communion with God (i.e., spiritual perfection).

THE NEO-ARISTOTELIANISM OF MAIMONIDES

Moses Maimonides, the Spaniard, is considered the foremost intellectual figure in medieval Judaism. Among Jewish medieval philosophers Maimonides was often referred to simply as "the philosopher." Although Maimonides believed that Aristotle had reached a high degree of intellectual perfection open to man, he was quick to note contradictions between the teachings of Aristotelian philosophy and the literal sense of the Bible. The Jewish scholars who were versed in biblical and rabbinical lore as well as in science and philosophy were perplexed. To guide the perplexed, Maimonides wrote in 1190 A.D. *The Guide of the Perplexed.* Throughout his Guide, the position of Maimonides has been that of the classical exponent of rationalism in Jewish religious philosophy. He believed in the power of the human mind to grasp metaphysical truth, and that metaphysics could only be understood through philosophical interpretations. Maimonides' first philosophic topic is God. The following is a brief summary of his theology.

God in Maimonides' Principles of Faith

Like Aristotle, Maimonides maintained that God exists, is a unity, and has no body. In Maimonides' *Commentary to the Mishneh,* he formulates his Thirteen Principles of Faith. His first principle is as follows: I believe with perfect faith that God is the Creator and ruler of all things. He alone has made, does make, and will make all things. In his commentary, Maimonides elaborates on this principle by maintaining that God is the Being, perfect in every possible way, who is the ultimate Cause of all existence. It is inconceivable that God does not exist, for if He did not exist, everything else would also cease to exist and nothing would remain. Maimonides maintains that the Torah itself teaches this first principle of faith in the first of the Ten Commandments (Exodus 20:2): "I am the Lord your God."

His second principle states: I believe with perfect faith that God is One. There is no unity that is in any way like His. He alone is our God—He was, He is, and He will be. This principle involves the unity of God. God is not like any other single thinker, which can be divided into a number of elements. God is not even like the simplest physical thing, which is still infinitely divisible. Rather, God is One in a unique way. There is no other unity like His. The Torah itself teaches this second principle of faith when it says (Deuteronomy 6:4), "Hear O Israel, the Lord is our God, the Lord is One."

The third principle of faith of Maimonides states: I believe with perfect faith that God does not have a body. Physical concepts do not apply to Him. There is nothing whatsoever that resembles Him at all. This third principle maintains that God is totally nonphysical and that nothing associated with the physical can apply to God in any way. Thus, it cannot be said that God moves, rests, or exists in a given place. Things such as this can neither happen to Him, nor be part of His intrinsic nature. In answer to the question about places in the Bible where God is portrayed as walking, standing, speaking, and so forth, Maimonides clearly states that these are examples of the Bible speaking metaphorically. So for example, when the Bible states that "God spoke," it is being used figuratively to mean that "God willed." The Torah itself teaches this third principle of faith when it says (Deuteronomy 4:15) "You have not seen any image."

The fourth principle of faith of Maimonides states: I believe with perfect faith that God is first and last. This principle involves the absolute eternity of God. Nothing else shares God's eternal quality. This is discussed many times in the Bible, and the Torah teaches it when it says of God (Deuteronomy 33:27), "The eternal God is a refuge."

The fifth principle of faith states: I believe with perfect faith that it is only proper to pray to God. One may not pray to anyone or anything else. This principle teaches that God is the only one whom people may serve and praise. We may sing only of God's greatness and obey only God's commandments. This principle in essence forbids all forms of idolatry.

The sixth principle of faith states: I believe with perfect faith that all the words of the Prophets are true. This principle recognizes that there existed humans beings, called Prophets, to whom God communicated. These men and women had such lofty qualities and were able to achieve such great perfection that their souls became prepared to receive pure spiritual wisdom.

The seventh principle of faith states: I believe with perfect faith that the prophecy of Moses is absolutely true. He was the chief of all Prophets, both before and after him. This principle maintains that Moses, of all of the Prophets who ever lived, was able to attain the highest possible human level. He perceived the godly to a degree surpassing every human being who ever existed. Thus he was the greatest of the Prophets.

The eighth principle of faith states: I believe with perfect faith that the entire Torah that we now have is that which was given to Moses. This principle maintains that Moses wrote the Torah down, much like a secretary taking dictation. Every word we have today was given directly to Moses by God.

The ninth principle of faith states: I believe with perfect faith that the Torah will not be changed, and that there will never be another Torah given by God. This principle involves permanence. That is to say, the Torah is God's permanent word, and no one else can change it. Nothing can be added to or subtracted from either the Written Torah or the Oral Torah. This is illustrated directly in the Torah when it states, "You shall not add to it, nor subtract from it" (Deuteronomy 13:1).

The tenth principle of faith states: I believe with perfect faith that God knows all of man's deeds and thoughts. It is thus written (Psalm 33:15), "He has molded every heart together, He understands what each does." This principle essentially maintains that God knows all that people do, and never turns His eyes away from them. However, Maimonides does maintain that people have absolute free will, and that God does not force them nor decree upon them what to do.

The eleventh principle states: I believe with perfect faith that God rewards those who keep His commandments, and punishes those who transgress His commandments. Maimonides states that the greatest possible reward is the World to Come, while the greatest possible punishment is being cut off from it. The Torah itself, Maimonides maintains, teaches this principle in the following account. Moses said to God (Exodus 32:32), "If You will, then forgive their sin, but if not, then extinguish me." God answered (Exodus 32:33), "The one who has sinned against Me, him will I erase from My book." This shows that God knows both the obedient and the sinner, rewarding one and punishing the other.

The twelfth principle states: I believe with perfect faith in the coming of the Messiah. No matter how long it takes, I will await his coming. This principle maintains that the Messiah will certainly come but that people should not set a time for his coming or try to calculate when he will come from scriptural passages.

The last and thirteenth principle of faith states: I believe with perfect faith that the dead will be brought back to life when God wills it to happen. The resurrection of the dead is one of the foundations handed down by Moses, and Maimonides maintains that one who does not believe in it cannot be associated with Judaism.

Proving God's Existence

Maimonides has argued that philosophic reasoning can prove the existence of God. He offers a number of arguments. Here is one of his arguments:

The universe is not empty. We can be certain that the things we perceive with our own senses exist. Existence of things can be explained in one of three ways: (1) all things are eternal and exist necessarily; (2) nothing is eternal and exists necessarily; (3) some things are eternal and exist necessarily, but some things are not. According to Maimonides, the first explanation is wrong, because we see things coming into existence at one time and disappearing at another. The second case is also wrong. If nothing were permanent, it is conceivable that everything might perish and nothing take its place, leaving an empty universe. Maimonides sees this as an absurdity, and therefore maintains that a necessary Being is needed to insure that the universe does not become depleted. This Being cannot derive its existence from an external source, because if it did, its existence would no longer be necessary. It would owe its existence to something else. Thus, the necessary Being must be totally independent of all else. Maimonides believed that it is impossible for two things each to exist independently, because they would then have to share a common essence: independent existence. To the degree they shared it, they would be part of a large whole and no longer independent. Therefore, Maimonides concludes that only one Being derives itself existence from itself, and this Being is God. Since God is self-caused, everything that derives its existence from an external source must ultimately derive its existence from God.

In a second proof, Maimonides maintains that any physical body will remain inert unless and until set in motion by some outside force. The universe consists of physical bodies in constant motion. What force is responsible for having started and maintaining them in motion? The Prime Mover (i.e., God) who alone possesses the power to move and make move without a preceding natural cause.

Maimonides' Negative Theology

In maintaining God's uniqueness, Maimonides states that the categories that are used to think about Him must also be unique and unlike any others. It cannot, therefore, be assumed that the grammatical structures that apply to finite objects like people also apply to God. Different subjects must be talked about in different ways. Correctly understood, a statement like "God is powerful" tells us not what God is but what God is

not. It says that God does not have any physical defi-
ciencies. In this way Maimonides turns all positive statements about God into negations, which separate the
idea of God and therefore preserve its unique identity.
In every case, Maimonides argues that God is radically
unlike people, which is the crux of what has come to be
termed "negative theology."

In conclusion, the only thing that people can really
say about God's nature is that it is off the scale of
intelligibility. God is beyond all human comprehension.

God's Angels

Maimonides firmly believed in the existence of angels,
who he perceived as pure intellects whose task it was to
act as messengers of God. Unlike Aristotle, who maintained that the angels were eternal and proceeded from
God, Maimonides held that it was God who created
them and put them in the governing forces.

God and Evil

Maimonides maintains that God is an all-good God, and
therefore rejects the possibility that God could be the
source of evil. For Maimonides, evil is the denial of the
good. It can be of the self-inflicted kind, as when people hurt and injure one another. Other forms of evil
exist because the world is made out of material matter,
which is subject to disintegration and decay.

In Summary

Maimonides, as a rationalist, was greatly influenced by
Aristotle. He believed that God is One, incorporeal,
eternal, and has given humankind an unchangeable

Torah of instruction. He further maintained that God is unknowable, and therefore everything written and said about God was done metaphorically in the language of people so that they would be able to understand.

In addition to its significance for medieval Jewish philosophy, Maimonides' works also have had a formative influence on modern Jewish thought. He provided a first acquaintance with philosophic speculation for a number of philosophers of the Enlightenment period and served as a bridge for the study of more modern philosophy.

THE MYSTICAL VIEW OF GOD—ISAAC LURIA

Jewish mysticism, or Kabbalah as it is known in Hebrew, is the form of Jewish religion that, through its esoteric teachings, seeks to cultivate personal communion between the worshiper and God. One of the distinguishing marks of Jewish mysticism is the intensity of religious feeling, rising frequently from ecstasy, which gives to it a dynamic force unknown to the ordinary religion.

Like other kinds of mysticism, Kabbalah draws upon the mystic's awareness of both the transcendence and immanence of God within the true religious life, every facet of which is a revelation of God. The second element of Kabbalah is that of theosophy, which seeks to reveal the hidden life of God and the relationships between the Divine life, on the one hand, and the life of man and creation, on the other. Judaism has a long history of mysticism, dating back to rabbinic times. However, the early Rabbis were not particularly supportive of mystic speculation, fearing that it could lead people away from Judaism.

It is believed that the *Zohar,* the *Book of Mystic Splendor,* was written late in the twelfth century. Its major aim was to explain God's commandments in a mystical way, dealing with the hidden meanings of the Bible. With the appearance of the *Zohar,* Jewish mysticism began to spread rapidly to European countries.

In the year 1492, the Jews of Spain were expelled, and the once great center of Jewish learning was in ruins. In the wake of this spiritual and physical upheaval, many Jews migrated to the Middle East. A number of them settled in the Upper Galilee, drawn to the town of Safed. It was here that a group of Jewish mystics were setting the stage for the numerous mystical movements of the next four hundred years, among them being the resurgence of interest in the study of Kabbalah.

Among the leaders of the Safed community was Rabbi Isaac Luria, often referred to as Ha-Ari (The Lion) from the Hebrew initials of the words *HaElohi Rabbi Yitchak* (The Divine Rabbi Isaac). He developed a new system for understanding the mysteries of the *Zohar.* It became known as the Lurianic method, and shed new light on the hidden wisdom of the Kabbalah.

The Kabbalistic God

Kabbalists maintain that God is unknowable to the human mind. They further believe that God is unlimited and infinite, and often refer to God as the *Ein Sof* (The Infinite One).

The kabbalistic system teaches that God is manifested or revealed through Divine *sefirot,* luminaries or spheres from which God emanated. The order of the spheres are: *keter* (crown); *chochmah* (wisdom), the first real manifestation of God, containing the ideal plan of all the worlds; *binah* (understanding), that is, Divine intelligence in which the hidden pattern achieves concreteness; *chesed* (mercy) from which flow the merciful qualities of God; *gevurah* (power), the source of Divine judgment and law; *tiferet* (beauty), mediating between *chesed* and *gevurah* to bring harmony and compassion upon the world; *netzach* (eternity); *hod* (majesty); *yesod* (foundation), which concentrates all the higher power and influences; and *malchut* (kingdom), the receptive or "female" potency that distributes the Divine stream to the lower worlds.

Meditation, prayer, study, and contemplation are ways for kabbalists to come to gain knowledge about God and how God relates to the world.

Doctrine of *Tzimtzum, Shevirat HaKelim,* and *Tikkun*

One of Luria's greatest contributions to Jewish thought was his doctrine of the three stages of creation. The following is a summary of that doctrine:

1. *Tzimtzum* (contraction): Since God was everywhere, Luria wondered how it was possible that there was space for anything to coexist with God. This question led Luria to the doctrine of *tzimtzum,* which means withdrawal or retreat. According to Luria, God contracted Himself and withdrew in order for the world itself to exist. By this act of withdrawal, God made room for the world by retreating from a portion of His universe. By retreating, God gave people the

freedom to exist on their own and to choose between good and evil. Why did God create a world in which evil was even a possibility? Why did God not create a world that was perfectly good? The next two parts of Isaac Luria's theory were attempts to answer these questions.

2. *Shevirat HaKelim* (breaking of the vessels): Luria used myths and symbols to explain his theory. The story that Luria told was a myth that attempted to explain why God had allowed the terrible suffering and tragedy of exile from Spain that occurred in 1492. Luria's myth was called "the breaking of the vessels." According to his myth, there is a flaw in the world. The reason for the flaw lies in what happened after God withdrew to allow the creation of the world. God created and destroyed many worlds. The first worlds that God created were destroyed because the light that came forth from God was too strong and powerful for people. The first worlds that God created after His retreat were called vessels. The destruction of these worlds was called "the breaking of the vessels." This cosmic catastrophe preceded the creation of our world.

Because of this accident, the world we live in is imperfect. Broken fragments of these vessels have fallen into our world. These broken vessels, called *kelippot* (shells) are symbolic of evil. Evil breaks the order of the world, and everything in the world became a series of broken fragments. The exile of the Jews from Spain was like the broken fragments, having moved the Jewish people from their place. The whole world, as Luria saw it, was flawed. It was not the way it ought to be.

3. *Tikkun* (repair of the world): Luria believed that God intended the world to be good. But since man had

the right to choose, evil was a possibility, and that is why God allowed the breaking of the vessels to occur. But God also gave man the power to combat evil. Sparks of light are symbolic of God's presence, and Luria believe that sparks of God's presence existed in the world. However, these Divine sparks were imprisoned in the *kelippot,* the broken fragments of the vessels. It is the task of the Jew, according to Luria, to free these scattered sparks from their shells and to reunite them with God.

This myth thus gave purpose to the suffering of the exiled Spanish Jews. The purpose of the exile was to extract the last sparks of godliness and to find the good within the world. By searching for God, man can restore and repair the world to its original state of harmony. The process of mending the world is called *tikkun.* Mending of the world can be accomplished through the performance of the *mitzvot*—God's commandments. The repair of the world can also be accomplished through prayer. True prayer, rendered with proper concentration and intention, says Luria, will allow a person's soul to ascend to and commune with God. The sign that complete *tikkun* has occurred will be the coming of the Messiah.

In Summary

Mysticism, although discouraged by the early rabbinic thinkers, has continued to shine its influence upon Jewish thinkers. For mystics, God exists, is unknowable, unlimited, and infinite. The ten emanations of God, known as *sefirot,* provide the bridge to the gap between the unknowable God and the known universe.

Isaac Luria preferred a world where man was free to choose, even if this meant the possibility of evil. His theory of God's contraction allows room for physical things in the world. The mission of the Jewish people is to help to mend the world (through performance of God's commandments) by gathering the Divine sparks that have been shattered and scattered throughout the universe. The complete repair of the world will hasten the coming of the Messiah.

THE BRIDGE TO MODERNISM—
BARUCH SPINOZA

Modern Jewish philosophy shared with Hellenistic and medieval Jewish philosophy a concern for relating general philosophy to Judaism. It did, however, differ from Hellenistic and medieval Jewish philosophy in several ways. For one thing, it differed in its conception of Jewish tradition. For Hellenistic and medieval Jewish philosophy, Judaism, with its oral and written law, was the revealed word of God, which was forever binding on the people. While some modern Jewish thinkers accepted this traditionalist opinion, most considered Judaism a creation of human thought.

One of the greatest philosophers of the entire western philosophic tradition was Baruch Spinoza. His passion for philosophy, which included his questioning of the Torah authorship of Moses, the denial of belief in the immortality of the soul, and his belief that God only exists philosophically, led to his excommunication from the Jewish community of Amsterdam in which he was raised. Though treated as a pariah by the Jews, he did not join any other religious group.

His work entitled *Theologico-Political Treatise* initiated modern Bible criticism. In another work, entitled *Ethics,* he proposes that a rational institution is the highest degree of knowledge, and argues that God and the universe are one and the same substance.

God's Nature

Spinoza's pantheistic theology maintained that God and the universe are one. God is nature, the laws of nature were set by God, and everything follows their structure. God does not act independently of the world, for God is the world. If God or nature is the only substance, everything else is understood in terms of Him, and is deducible from His essence.

God for Spinoza is not a purposeful being. There are no goals being achieved. God just is, and due to His being, everything happens, and happens of necessity. Man's ultimate aim is the intellectual love of God, which can give man the continuous and unending happiness that was sought. Thus the philosophical goal of complete wisdom becomes man's salvation.

Body and Mind

For Spinoza, everything is in God, who is modified in terms of His two known attributes, thought and extension. The world of body and of mind are two aspects of God or Nature. The order and connection of ideas is the same as the order and connection of things. The latter can be understood in terms of mathematical physics, the former in terms of logic and psychology, but both are ways of understanding the same substance, God. Thus the mind and the body are essentially the same thing.

Knowledge

For Spinoza, man, through the course of experience, develops general ideas of what is going on in the world, and through these, a level of scientific understanding of the sequence of events taking place. From these man comes to adequate ideas, which gives him a logical understanding. The highest form of knowledge, according to Spinoza, would be to have a complete understanding, to see everything as a logical system from the aspect of eternity. This intuitive knowledge is only completely possessed by God. Complete understanding would be to know the infinite idea of God, which man can only approach but never fully know.

In Summary

Spinoza's totally rationalistic vision incorporates several basic Jewish themes: the existence and unity of God, the dependence of everything on God, and the love of God being the highest good. His view, however, is considered to be the first modern one to provide a metaphysical basis for rejecting any form of Judaism or Christianity portraying the human scene as an interplay between man and God. The denial of any distinction between God and the world and the possibility of any supernatural events or revelatory knowledge eliminated the basic ingredients of a Jewish or Christian cosmology. Spinoza's pantheistic outlook instead offered the basis for a completely secular and naturalistic understanding of the universe.

Spinoza has been described as "the most impious atheist that ever lived on the face of the earth" and also a "God-intoxicated man." His theory provides the foundation for a kind of atheism in which the interrelationship of God and man is denied, and in which God has no personality whatsoever. His revolutionary steps replaced religious tradition by rational, scientific study. His main influence was on biblical critics, Deists, and eighteenth-century French atheists, and his ideas have even been seen as precursors of Marxism.

MOSES MENDELSSOHN

Moses Mendelssohn was an eighteenth-century philosopher of the German Enlightenment and spiritual leader of German Jewry. As a philosopher of religion, he did not create an original system. Rather he continued in the tradition of the classical rationalism of the seventeenth and eighteenth centuries. His philosophy incorporates the themes of reason as the medium by which man acquires knowledge, that man is endowed with eternally valid ideas of absolute goodness and truth, and the purpose of philosophy as the achievement of happiness through the perfection of man.

The starting point of Mendelssohn's philosophy of religion is his theory of knowledge. He distinguishes between eternal truths, which are self-evident to reason, and historical, temporal truths, requiring the evidence of sense experience. Among the eternal truths are the belief in a wise and merciful God and the immortality of the human soul. These metaphysical truths are the themes of his two major works, *Morgenstunden*

(1785) and *Phaedon* (1767). In the former he seeks to demonstrate the rationality of the belief in the existence of God and treats the subject as a principle of man's universal religion of reason. In his work entitled *Phaedon,* Mendelssohn deals with the immortality of the soul.

God's Existence

Mendelssohn's favorite proof for God's existence is a modification of the ontological argument: Man finds the idea of a Supreme Being in his consciousness. Since this idea cannot have arisen out of man's limited experiences, we have no direct knowledge of anything remotely resembling the idea of Divine perfection—it is *a priori* and belongs to the category of concepts that precede all experience and enable us to comprehend the universe. Although these concepts do not arise from experience, they are not subjective because they determine the character of universal experience. Further, there is a necessary connection between the concept of a perfect being and his existence. A being that is absolutely perfect must have existence among its attributes.

Immortality of the Soul

Mendelssohn maintained that an infinite number of souls constitute the inner substance of the universe. Things that perish do not cease to exist. Rather, they are dissolved into their elements. The soul is such an element, and is neither weakened by age or destroyed by death. That the soul will retain its consciousness in a future state is guaranteed by the goodness of God, who has implanted in man the idea that the soul is immortal.

Man's Freedom of Choice

Mendelssohn differs with Jewish tradition regarding free will for man. Inasmuch as every act of will must have a cause, human freedom, if defined as an uncaused act, is logically impossible. Man's will can be free only in the sense that it is determined by a recognition of the good. But if man is not truly free, the sinner cannot be responsible for his deeds. If this be the case, then why, Mendelssohn asks, should he be punished? To this question Mendelssohn responds that Divine punishment is not an end in itself, but a means of purging sinners in order to prepare them for the future world to come.

In Summary

According to Mendelssohn, the world is to be regarded as detached from God, in addition to its immanent existence within God—according to the pantheistic outlook of Spinoza. This enables Mendelssohn to uphold the concept of the creation of the world by God and Divine providence, which metes out reward and punishment. This, according to Mendelssohn, was the basis of moral conduct. Mendelssohn was compelled to dissociate himself from Spinoza's attitude toward Judaism. Although both he and Spinoza sought to liberate religion from the coercive measure employed by the state, Mendelssohn also called for the avoidance of coercive measures within the realm of religion itself. Mendelssohn became a legend even during his own lifetime, and he was regarded by many as the embodiment of the humanist ideal.

THE TWENTIETH CENTURY: MARTIN BUBER
AND HIS DIALOGICAL PHILOSOPHY

The twentieth century brought many different and important influences in Jewish thought, which gave it a dynamic new direction. Especially notable was the existentialist school under the influence of Soren Kierkegaard, the great Danish theologian, which stressed the significance of personal existence against abstract philosophy. This provided Jewish thinkers, such as Martin Buber, with a different vantage point from which to view the relation between philosophy and religion.

Western Europe of the late nineteenth century was permeated with new cultural and intellectual currents. Buber ventured into this world in search of knowledge, meaning, and direction. He soon became disenchanted with the conventional European philosophies, which did not touch his soul or give him direction. The only movement that truly affected him and transformed him into a universalist and humanist was the relatively new school of thought and approach to life—the existential philosophy.

Existentialism was the new intellectual child of that era and culture. Existentialist philosophers maintained that man need not go far to search for solutions to problems such as human suffering in the world. They claimed that the solution lies within man himself. Man need not look for purpose in the universe, because the universe has no purpose. It is only man who has purpose, and the meaning for man's life is to be found within man himself. So it is with truth, which is not absolute nor does it reside outside of man. Truth can only be found within man himself, in his soul. The same holds true for reality. The real world is not the ideal or the abstract world. It is our existing world, the world of today that is of utmost importance.

A major influence on Buber was the German philosopher Friedrich Nietzche and the Danish Kierkegaard. They nurtured Buber's thirsty soul. From them he learned that every person must seek his or her own pathway to God, and that building faith in God on sheer historical grounds is a fatal delusion.

I-Thou

Among Buber's books is one entitled *I-Thou*. It is in this book that Buber presents his entire philosophy.

Buber's philosophy is built on the concept of unity. Man's greatest achievement in life, he claims, is the attainment of unity: unity within the single man, between man and man, unity among the segments of a nation, unity among nations, unity between mankind and the inanimate world, and unity between the universe and God. This unity is basically spiritual in nature and is achieved by building spiritual bridges between man and man, between man and nature, and between man and his spiritual world. Buber proposes his "I-Thou" dialogue as an instrument for the attainment of this unity.

The world is bipolar. Every subject is a subject in relationship to an object, and an object in relationship to a subject. There is no subject without an object, and there is no object without a subject. It is the relationship between the two that makes the subject and the object what they are. Thus, according to Buber's theory, what really exists between man and man, man and nature, and man and his spiritual world is a relationship, or more correctly, an attitude.

Buber spoke of two primary attitudes between man and his surrounding world: the "I-Thou" and the "I-It" attitudes. The basic words "I," "Thou," and "It," he explained, come in pairs, in which the two words relate to each other. The word "I" does not exist by itself nor do the words "Thou" and "It." They are intertwined into an "I-Thou" or "I-It" relationship. In order to accentuate the special meaning of these relationships, Buber deliberately ignored the common word "you" and instead introduced the word "Thou," which represents in his vocabulary uniqueness. By using the word "Thou," he wished to connote mutuality, directness, and familiarity. This was the same mutuality and directness between a living mother and her beloved child, between husband and wife in the passion of merged feelings and understanding, where the common word "you" does not suffice, and the personal familiar "thou" is required to indicate a binding relationship and an attitude of communion. The "I-Thou" relationship, according to Buber, represents the supreme level of relationship, which is exemplified through authentic communion and loss of consciousness.

While "I-Thou" is dialogue, "I-It" is monologue. "I-It" is one-sided, relating to man's confined physical and empirical world, to the world of things, to the world of use and experience. The "I-It" is a subject-object relationship. It is an attitude that is always indirect and treats even people as objects. This is a theory void of mutuality and communion. A table, a chair, a pencil, or even a messenger boy who happens to pass through an office are no more than things that happen to exist side by side without interrelationship and without mutuality with the person who happens to occupy the office.

Buber goes on to say that in the "I-Thou" relationship, the "I" can only maintain only fleeting glances with the "Thou." The "Thou" continually becomes an "It" and the "It" may occasionally become a "Thou" again. Buber presents an example of such a relationship between the "I" and "Thou": A child, lying in bed with its eyes half closed, waits with a tense soul for its mother to speak to it, anxiously desires to communicate with her. The mother arrives, they glance at each other, their eyes shining with love. This, to Buber, is an experience of communion and mutuality. But this mutuality is often short-lived. Soon the same child views its mother just like any other object. Now the child no more calls her and neither does the mother answer. The "Thou" has been replaced by the "It."

Man can choose to live entirely in the world of "It" and forever securely do so, but the consequence of this choice is pathetic—man ceases to be man.

Buber explains that the "I-Thou" relationship exists in all realms of life, and demonstrates its significance with examples from the world of nature, people, and the world of the intellect.

God, the Eternal Thou

Buber's analysis of the "I-Thou" relation leads him to his notion of God as the Eternal Thou and to his description of the relation between man and God as an "I-Thou" relation. God, the Eternal Thou, is known not through cognitive propositions or through metaphysical speculation, but through one's particular "I-Thou" relationships with persons, animals, and nature. The meetings with the Eternal Thou constitute revelation. Thus for Buber, revelation is not only something that happened many years ago at Mount Sinai, but something that happens in the present, through a person's life, if one is open to receive it. For Buber, the Bible itself is simply a record of the dialogical encounters between man and God. Since the laws of the Bible are only the human response to revelation, they are therefore not binding on later generations.

God's Covenant with Israel

The dialogue between God and the Israelites is epitomized in the covenant, which lies at the basis of Jewish messianism. God, Buber states, demands that the Israelites become a holy people, thereby making the real kingship of God in every aspect of communal life. For Buber, the essence of the religious life is not one's affirmation of religious beliefs, but the way in which one meets the challenges of everyday life.

In Summary

Martin Buber introduced a new way of thinking about relating to others. His "I-Thou" philosophical theory has also had a strong influence on modern Jewish educators. He not only viewed education from an existential viewpoint, but established an extensive existential philosophy of education that corresponds to his "I-Thou" dialogic philosophy. Buber emphasized the spiritual qualities of the teacher—personality, characters, commitment to scholarship, and empathy with his students and their needs. He also proposed a curriculum based on his "I-Thou" philosophical theory that would teach students to transcend their selves and their national welfare, and learn to integrate themselves with their families, their immediate society, their nation, and with humankind at large. Several educators have even considered Buber's philosophy to be the intellectual ancestor and the ideological blueprint of the authentic modern open school.

THE NEO-KANTIANISM OF HERMANN COHEN

This German philosopher gave up initial plans to become a rabbi and instead turned to philosophy. His early works were devoted primarily to an evaluation of idealism as embodied in the thought of Plato and Kant. These words, which included *Kant's Theory of Experience,* brought Cohen to a new interpretation of Kant's philosophy, which came to be known as the Marburg School of neo-Kantianism. This approach found expression in works entitled *The Logic of Pure Knowledge, The Ethics of the Pure Will,* and *The Aesthetic of Pure Feelings.* These works reflected Cohen's contention that philosophy's three main branches are logic, ethics, and aesthetics, which investigate the underlying assumptions of the basic modes of consciousness—thinking, willing, and feeling, respectively.

Ethics and the Idea of God

For Cohen, the idea of God played a central role in ethics, which provided mankind with an eternal idea. If mankind were to cease to exist, there would be no possibility of achieving the ethical ideal. It is here that Cohen introduces his concept of God, whose function it is to guarantee the eternity of the world, and thus the fulfillment of the moral ideal. Cohen's conception of God was quite different from the personal God of traditional Judaism. For Cohen, God was an idea or concept rather than an existent being.

The New God Idea of Cohen

At age seventy, when he moved from Marburg to Berlin, his contact with the Jews in Vilna and Warsaw brought a marked change in his concept of God. Cohen maintained that there are problems that ethics cannot explain. Although ethics is concerned with man in general, it does not take into account the personal concerns of the individual. Whereas the Early Prophets judged the world from the general ethical standpoint, the Later Prophets (Jeremiah, Isaiah, and Ezekiel) are very concerned with the individual. Cohen identified prophetic Judaism with the highest spiritual insight of the Jewish people and with ethical monotheism (a concept of the unity of God grounding moral responsibility).

Cohen's new attitude found its expression in his work *The Religion of Reason from the Sources of Judaism,* which was published posthumously by his wife. This book clearly shows that Cohen had abandoned his belief that reality is rooted in human reason and now maintained that reality is rooted in God with man's reason itself originating in God. For Cohen, God was no longer an idea, but a pure Being while the world was becoming.

Relative to the question that now arises concerning how a world that is becoming could possibly exist beside God who is eternal being, Cohen develops the new concept of "correlation." Being and becoming are connected to one another insofar as one concept logically requires the other. That is to say, becoming could not exist if there were no eternal existence (i.e., God) who could endow it with power. On the other hand, being could not exist without becoming, and the existence of God would have no meaning without creation.

Cohen maintained that the correlation between God and man is characterized by the Holy Spirit (*ruach hakodesh*), which is an attribute of the relation between God and man. The Holy Spirit binds man and God together, and the correlation between man and God is manifest in man's attempt to imitate God, the source of all holiness, and to become holy himself. Man's specific creative mission is to help all people live in peace and harmony, which will bring about the messianic era.

God's Commandments

Following Immanuel Kant and his doctrine of morality (which maintains that an action is moral if it is performed from a sense of duty and is autonomous), Cohen interprets God's command (i.e., *mitzvah*) to mean both "law" and "duty." The law originates in God, while the sense of duty originates in people. God issued commandments to man, and man, of his own free will, takes upon himself the so-called "yoke of the commandments." With the "yoke of the commandments,'' man simultaneously accepts the ''yoke of the kingship of God.''

In Summary

Cohen's influence on other Jewish intellectuals was profound. He argued that within Judaism, one finds represented the correct understanding of the dynamic relationship between man and God. This new appraisal of the relation of Judaism to philosophy and Cohen's demand that religion was not to be subordinated to philosophical demands revolutionized Jewish thought. Franz Rosenzweig and Martin Buber were especially influenced by Cohen, particularly his concept of correlation, which became the source of much of the dialogical relationship of God and man.

LEO BAECK

Hermann Cohen had likely foreseen that the Jewish thinker most likely to carry on his work was Leo Baeck, a German rabbi and thinker who drew heavily on the Jewish thought of Cohen. He was a philosophical thinker of wide general knowledge, a preacher, and a historian of religion. He was also the only modern Jewish theologian to enter and survive the concentration camps.

Nature of God

As opposed to Hermann Cohen, Baeck argues that the idea of God has little more religious value than any other pure idea. The certainty that God is real does not derive from a rational demonstration that God is the

First Cause in the universe, but rather in what has happened in peoples' lives, in the sense of meaning and direction that they have. For Baeck, God is not to be understood as a God of qualities or about whom dogmas may be listed. However, Judaism is well aware that since people are conscious of God as One who is responsive to people, God can be understood personally and regarded as personal.

Baeck further maintains that there is a fundamental paradox about God as presented in Judaism. On the one hand, God is a transcendent God—exalted and Sovereign King. On the other hand, God is a personal God—Our Father and Parent. Thus the ethical and the devotional are simultaneously affirmed in Judaism. God can be personally sensed but still retains His quality of being an ethically demanding God.

Mysteries and Commandments

Baeck viewed the essence of Judaism as a dialectical polarity between "mystery" and "command." The commands, according to Baeck, do not necessarily form a system of commandments like the established *halachah* (system of Jewish law), which imposes a fixed and very directed way of life. Rather, they appear from time to time in the form of instructions for action like lightning bolts that break through the clouds covering the Divine "mystery." Baeck continued to adhere to Hermann Cohen's interpretation of Judaism as "ethical monotheism." He believed that piety is achieved by the fulfillment of the duties between man and man, and that even observances through ritual are directed toward this ethical aim.

God and Evil

As previously mentioned, Baeck was the only major modern Jewish theologian to enter and survive the death camps. With regard to his theory of evil, Baeck maintains that the source of evil is the misuse of human freedom. People are responsible for creating evil in the world, and not God. However, people who have committed wrongs can and often do change their ways and make themselves once again acceptable to God. They do this through repentance (*teshuvah,* in Hebrew). For Baeck, people must always take responsibility for what they do. The power to do good or evil is in the hands of humankind.

In Summary

There has been lasting greatness to Baeck's thought, especially in his reaffirming the right of religion to speak to the heart. Although reason and rationalism appealed to so many Jews of the time, Baeck persisted in upholding his belief that personal spirituality was always to be a part of the essence of Judaism.

FRANZ ROSENZWEIG

Franz Rosenzweig, a German Jewish theologian and friend and colleague of Martin Buber, is most noted for his near conversion out of Judaism to Christianity early in his career. When enacting his resolution at a High Holiday service in an Orthodox synagogue in Berlin, he had an experience that convinced him to reverse his decision. From this time onward, he stated that he intended to recover Judaism not only for himself, but for others like himself.

His major work, entitled *The Star of Redemption,* proposes to offer a philosophical theology of both Judaism and Christianity. The three parts of this work can be summarized as follows.

Book 1: Man, the Universe, and God

Rosenzweig regards the world as consisting of three elements—man, the universe, and God. According to the Bible, these three elements interact through the processes of creation, revelation, and redemption. Revelation is initiated by God as the process of relating, first God to man, and then man to God, and through his life to the world. Rosenzweig maintains that truth is subjective and arrived at by the individual on the basis of his own personal existence, and can be verified only in the life of the individual.

Book 2: Revelation of God

For Rosenzweig, revelation is not a single historical event (such as that which occurred atop Mount Sinai), but rather the continuous entry into relationship with man on the part of God. All religions are built on a revelatory experience. It takes a verbal form, with its content simply God's identification of Himself to people in love. God's love for man evokes a reciprocal love from man to God, which creates ties between the two, giving life meaning and ultimate direction. For Rosenzweig, the total content of God's revelation is God's self-disclosure, the fact of His presence and His concern for the Jewish people. By virtue of God's relation to people, God is involved in time and works in history. Thus, Rosenzweig's God is a personal God, very much like the one described in the Bible.

Rosenzweig parts company from his colleague Buber when it comes to understanding the relationship between revelation and Jewish law. Although both agree that law is not part of the content of revelation, Rosenzweig maintains that the sense of "being commanded" is a part of revelation's content.

Book 3: Search for the Kingdom of God

Rosenzweig maintains that man's desire in prayer and action for the permanent reality of the revelatory experience in community is the search for the kingdom of God. The Jewish people entered into this kingdom from the outset and must continue to live through the Jewish calendar and Judaism's liturgy, always maintaining its special covenantal relationship with God.

In Summary

Rosenzweig's writings and thoughts have exerted a significant influence on theologians, including Heschel and Maybaum. In the *Commentary Symposium* of 1965, Rosenzweig was credited by the modern Jewish thinkers polled with being the most influential modern Jewish thinker. To this day, his thought stands on its own as a special example of Jewish existentialism.

MORDECAI KAPLAN'S NATURALISM

Mordecai Kaplan, a twentieth-century rabbi, was the founder of America's fourth stream of Judaism—Reconstructionism. In his writings, he combined scholarship with creative application of the texts to contemporary problems.

In his important work, *Judaism as a Civilization,* he defined Judaism as an evolving religious civilization, maintaining that as a civilization the Jewish people possess all the characteristics of land, political organization, and culture subsumed under that designation. By "religious," Kaplan means that Jewish civilization expresses itself best by clarifying the purposes and values of human existence, in wrestling with God (conceived in nonpersonal terms) and in the ritual of home, synagogue, and community. However, because Judaism is a civilization, the secular elements of culture are essential to Jewish spirituality and help to curb the tendency of religion toward rigidity.

By "evolving," Kaplan means that Judaism should be considered from a practical, historical point of view, rather than a metaphysical one. Thus, the focus of the content of Jewish life must be the Jewish people and its needs, rather than revealed texts. In his naturalistic approach, Kaplan believed that the Jewish people must cherish diversity.

Nature of God

Kaplan's revisionist theology emerged as he began to ask himself some difficult questions. For example, if the Torah is a composite of different documents with internal contradictions, then in what way is it the word of God? And if it is not the word of God, then wherein lies its authority? Kaplan's naturalistic view of God was based on the proposition that the world can be explained scientifically using verifiable ideas. Thus Kaplan regards God as that power in the universe on which man must rely for the achievement of his destiny. God for Kaplan was a power or process that pervades all things. And the Torah was the medium through which the presence of God was revealed in people and in nature at large.

For Kaplan, belief in God constituted a program of action for people. Since God is the power that makes for good and truth in the world, then whenever people display moral responsibility, they manifest the presence of God. Unlike Spinoza's pantheistic philosophy, which maintained that God Himself was synonymous with the universe, Kaplan's religious naturalism portrayed God as that aspect of the world that brings humans fulfillment and salvation.

God and the Prayer Book

Since God is a process according to Kaplan, it is reasonable to conclude that Kaplan has a unique understanding of the purpose of prayer vis-à-vis God. For Kaplan, the purpose of prayer is to assist people in strengthening the forces and relationships by which they fulfill themselves as persons. It is not important to Kaplan that one's prayers actually be "heard." Rather, prayer provides the opportunity for worshipers to voice their desires and yearnings to achieve their goals, which in their totality spell God. In viewing prayer in this manner, one should not, according to Kaplan, expect one's prayers to change or alter natural events in the world.

In Summary

Kaplan replaced the traditionalist supernatural God of classical Jewish religion with the God of modern, naturalist religion. God is not, for Kaplan, a separate, independent Being existing beyond nature, but rather a power totally within the natural order of the universe. Revelation, for Kaplan, was simply the natural process by which human beings discover visions of an ever more perfect world order and strive to implement them. This naturalism represented a very different way of understanding what it means to be a religious Jew in the modern age. First and foremost on Kaplan's mind is the importance of the Jewish community, the people of Israel. When the community begins to grapple with all of the basic problems of individual and communal living and live moral and ethical lives, then God's presence will have been revealed.

Finally, Kaplan's notion of Judaism as a civilization led to the creation of the important American Jewish institution known as the Jewish Community Center, which combined within its walls arts, sports, study, and worship within a Jewish communal framework.

10

Jewish Theology since 1945

ABRAHAM JOSHUA HESCHEL

The search for an authentic contemporary Judaism is not a uniquely contemporary problem. One might argue that the search is as old as Judaism itself, that it is of the essence of the Prophets, of Rabbinic Judaism and medieval Jewish thought, of neo-Orthodox, Reform, Conservative, and Reconstructionist Judaism. This past in part creates our present. However, the actual situation addressed by and which addresses Jewish thinkers since 1945 has an unprecedented quality created by two transformative events in Jewish history: the Holocaust and the rebirth of the State of Israel. New theological questions emerge with these two events: "Where was God at Auschwitz?" "Is there a connection between the rebirth of the State of Israel and the Holocaust?" "Is God speaking to the Holocaust survivors through the State of Israel?"

With the rebirth of Israel, there is a new positiveness about Judaism even before the actual theological inquiry occurs. In this section, several modern post–World War II thinkers and their responses will be examined. The first is Abraham Joshua Heschel.

Heschel is the product of two different worlds. His life and work can best be understood as an attempt to achieve a synthesis between the traditional learning of Eastern European Jewry and the philosophy and scholarship of Western civilization. Although he died in 1972, he still continues to be one of the most influential philosophers of religion in the United States.

Heschel's works, including *Man Is Not Alone, Man's Quest for God,* and *God in Search of Man,* attempt to illuminate the underlying reality of religion, namely the living, dynamic relationship between man and God. Although he uses tools of modern philosophy, he is always sure to point out that rational analysis has its limitations when it comes to attempting to disclose the ineffable quality of the Divine.

Contemplating God

Heschel maintains that there are three starting points of contemplation about God. They include: sensing the presence of God in the world in things, in the Bible, and in sacred deeds. He bases these three trails to God on three verses in the Torah: "Lift up your eyes on high and see, who created these?" (Isaiah 40:26). "I am the Lord Your God" (Exodus 20:2). "We shall do and we shall hear" (Exodus 24:7).

Heschel maintains that these three ways correspond in Jewish tradition to the main aspects of religious existence: worship, learning, and action.

Heschel further argues that wonder or what he calls "radical amazement" is the chief characteristic of the religious person's attitude toward history and nature. Awareness of the Divine begins with wonder. The greatest hindrance to this awareness is to become so accustomed to life's marvels that they are taken for granted and become commonplace. On the other hand, being in awe of the beauty and the mysteries of the universe is to participate in the wisdom of God Himself.

Nature of God

Heschel maintained that nothing in Jewish life is more hallowed than the saying of the *Shema:* "Hear O Israel, the Lord is our God, the Lord is One." For Heschel this means that God is not only superior to any other being, but God is unique and incomparable. There is no equivalent of the Divine. Heschel also maintained that God is a Being who is both in nature and history, both love and power, near and far, known and unknown, Father and Eternal.

In his writings about God, Heschel constantly emphasizes that God is personally involved with the world and moved and affected by all things that happen in society. It is the biblical God's reaching out of Himself and turning to man that Heschel characterizes as God's "pathos." For Heschel, the Bible was a serious important document, meant to be read carefully. Any careful reader of the Bible would find God's concern for humanity throughout its pages.

For Heschel, one of the ways to "reach" God is through prayer, which he often defined as "the opening of one's thoughts to God." Since he maintained that God cares about man and is always in search of him, prayer becomes the clearing of the path for His approach. Thus prayer helps bring man to God's attention to be listened to and to be understood by Him.

God's Commandments

Heschel maintains that the Torah and its laws were given to the Jews by God as a sign of God's love. To reciprocate that love, the Jews must strive to attain the love of Torah, demonstrated by the performance of both God's positive and negative commandments. For Heschel, all religious acts must be performed with a willing heart and proper intention (*kavanah*). In this way, a person cherishes the law, rather than just complying with it. The ultimate aim for people is to be, as Heschel puts it, an "incarnation of the Torah." In this way, the Torah and its laws are in man, his soul, and in his deeds.

In Summary

Heschel defines religion itself as "the answer to man's ultimate questions." Since people today are largely alienated from the reality that informs genuine religion, Heschel tries to recover the salient existential questions to which Judaism offers the answers. This leads to a theology of a God who is not some philosophical abstraction but rather a living entity that is concerned and cares about His creatures. Observance of God's demands with proper intention and love and praying with true feelings are important routes to God's reality and man's fulfillment.

MILTON STEINBERG

Milton Steinberg, an American Conservative rabbi, was concerned with a philosophical approach to Judaism. His works, including *Basic Judaism, As a Driven Leaf, A Believing Jew,* and *Anatomy of Faith,* all dealt with important theological issues, including the nature of God, God's relation to man and history, the problem of evil, and the confrontation of faith and reason.

Nature of God

Steinberg maintains, like many other theologians, that human knowledge about God must be limited because of the limitations of the human mind. He therefore argues that God's existence can only be accepted based on faith alone.

Steinberg maintains, much like Mordecai Kaplan, that God is both a Single Power and a Mind, much like the human mind. God is an ethical God and enters into relationships with people.

Steinberg readily admits that God is all-good but not all-powerful, arriving at the conclusion that people have free will, which limits God's power. This kind of "limited theism," in which evil exists and God is powerless to overcome it, holds that evil represents the lower stages of reality out of which humankind emerged. Thus for Steinberg, the elements of chance within the universe absolve God, so to speak, from the evil present in the world.

God's Relationship to Man

Steinberg maintains that since there is evil and imperfection in the world and God is self-limited, both God and man need to bond together in order to face the task of eradicating imperfection. Humanity then becomes God's co-worker, in order to face the challenges of imperfect things in the world together.

In Summary

Steinberg's limited theism is based on a God that is believed to be all-good, but self-limiting and not all-powerful. This explains the reason why evil pervades the world. He further argues that it is impossible to prove rationally with one hundred percent certainty the existence of God in the universe. Rather, one must have faith in a universe that is dynamic and rational, and whose order would likely posit a unique Power essential to all beings.

Since God is not all-powerful, evil exists in the world because humans were given free will. The challenge ahead is for both man and God to join forces in order to fight the source of evil and bring greater light into the world.

THEOLOGY AFTER THE HOLOCAUST

Jewish life and thought have been radically transformed by the Holocaust. The tragedy of the Holocaust and the incredible number of lost lives have left Jewish thinkers numb and many people with challenges to their very faith in God.

The question of why there is evil in the world is as old in Judaism as the God-faith itself. Since no generation and no individual has been spared the painful necessity of justifying God's way, the answers throughout the centuries have been quite varied. Here is a brief summary of the various answers in a search for an acceptable "theodicy" (i.e., an explanation of evil that will reconcile the fact of it with the existence of God).

Moral Theories

1. Evil is the result of some prior sin of the person on whom it was visited.
2. Evil may represent the expiation of the transgression of a community rather than the individual (i.e., individuals are held responsible for the sins of their community).
3. Evil is necessary for goodness and morality to exist.
4. Evil is indispensable to man's character, since, were it not for its prodding, no one would ever bestir himself or develop attachments to justice and compassion.

Metaphysical Theories

1. Evil has no reality in itself but is merely the absence of good.
2. Evil only appears as evil because it is seen isolated or in a partial view.

Evil Is Temporary

1. Evil will be compensated and made good in the life after one's life.

2. Evil represents the survival into the human condition of other lower stages of reality out of which humans have emerged. The traces of evil are constantly being erased with time until the day when people will be perfectly human.

Evil Is Inscrutable

Evil is and always will remain a mystery, known only to God alone. This is the moral ending of the Book of Job, which states that it is not in our power to explain either the tranquility of the wicked or the sufferings of the upright.

Judaism has never promulgated one single authoritative "official" theodicy. It has always postulated choices, and expects people always to recognize evil as something that needs to be combatted.

THEODICY: THEOLOGIANS' RESPONSES TO EVIL IN THE WORLD

The focus of all theological speculation about the place of evil in the world is its relationship to God. The dilemma is: If God is all-powerful, then He is in some way responsible for evil. If God is not responsible, then God is not all-powerful. In that case, evil exists independently of God and God's sovereignty is challenged. Thus the choice lies between these two options: an all-powerful God who is responsible for evil or a limited God who is not.

This section will present various theologians and their specific responses to the problem of evil, pain, and suffering in the world.

Richard Rubenstein

Richard Rubenstein, an American rabbi, was a controversial theologican highly influenced by the so-called death of God school in contemporary Christian theology. This movement developed in the 1960s as a Christian theological response to that era's sense of religious alienation, the constant presence of evil in society, and God's seeming indifference to it. Rubenstein's writings reflected his position that the horror of the Holocaust represented a radically new phenomenon that required a radical response.

Rubenstein's "Death of God" Theology

The "death of God" phrase resonates with Christological overtones. Jesus had to die in order to accomplish his Divine mission, and his death allows for the vicarious atonement of human sins.

Rubenstein maintains that God Himself did not die, but rather the human conception of God has died. The statement "God has died" means that after an experience as cruel and horrific as the Holocaust, one cannot any longer speak about a personal God who is all-powerful, loving, caring, and compassionate.

Rubenstein replaces the traditional conception of God as caring and loving with a return to the mystical God who is totally undefinable and the source of all creation to which all creation ultimately returns.

Paradoxically, Rubenstein argues that in the age of the "death of God," people need religion with its rituals and traditions in order to deal with the many crises in their lives. The community of Israel is very important, and people need each other in order to create meaning in their lives. Judaism should continue as a means of helping individual Jews meet life's inevitable traumas.

Although Rubenstein's radical theology failed to strike deep roots into the less traditional Jewish theologians, his writings have given us a powerful image of what it means to draw the extreme conclusion that "God is dead."

Emil Fackenheim

No theologian has written as extensively about the Holocaust as Emil Fackenheim, a Canadian rabbi and himself a survivor of the Holocaust. In his book *God's Presence in History,* he has tried to find a way to avoid the faith of the pious who see no special problem in the Holocaust, and those like Rubenstein, who argue for God's death.

Fackenheim adamantly refuses to allow any theological explanation to be given of the Holocaust. In this sense, the Holocaust for him is devoid of any meaning and an absurdity. Yet, despite all of this, Fackenheim calls on people to believe and affirm the continued existence of God in Jewish history. Auschwitz for Fackenheim becomes revelation! Jews learn that they are under a sacred obligation to survive, and therefore are forbidden to despair of the God of Israel and His redemptive powers. Thus, for Fackenheim, every Jew who has remained a Jew since 1945 has responded affirmatively to the commanding voice of Auschwitz. And the rebirth of the State of Israel in 1948 is living testimony to God's continued saving presence in history. According to Fackenheim, nothing else the Jews have done so fully sums up and projects the Jewish people's rejection of death and return to life.

Eliezer Berkovits

Eliezer Berkovits is a modern Orthodox theologian whose seminal work is *Faith After the Holocaust*. He presents a more traditional response to the Holocaust, and also explores various historic responses to suffering in Jewish tradition.

Berkovits cannot understand why so many Jewish thinkers insist that God was not to be found in the death camps. In fact, he states, many found that God was available to help them bear their suffering.

It is this premise and his calling people's attention to the common saints and everyday heroes of the death camps upon which his theology is based. Calling attention to a biblical response of evil in the Bible—the notion of *hester panim* ("Hiding Face of God")—Berkovits maintains that at times God mysteriously and without cause hides from man. God's hiding from man, Berkovits maintains, is required for man to be a moral creature. God's hiddenness creates the possibility of human action. This is a reiteration of the classic view that free will is necessary for morality to exist. With God's power limited, human moral action becomes all the more important if the world is to be redeemed. Like Fackenheim, Berkovits declares that the rebirth and continued existence of Israel despite its centuries of suffering is the greatest single proof that God is present in history despite His hiddenness.

Ignaz Maybaum

Ignaz Maybaum is an English Reform rabbi who sought the meaning of the Holocaust from within the traditional Jewish responses to suffering. Unlike Rubenstein and Fackenheim, Maybaum views Auschwitz not as a unique event in Jewish history, but as a reappearance of a classic, sanctified event.

In his seminal work *The Face of God after Auschwitz,* Maybaum affirms the dynamic relation of God and Israel, believing in the reality of a transcendent God who made a covenant with the Israelites. Israel is unique among the nations, its history always being played out in relation to other peoples and empires.

Maybaum, conscious of Israel's relation to the gentiles, classifies the event of the Holocaust as a *churban* (destruction)—an event like that of the destruction of the Jerusalem Temple, which ends an old era and creates a new one. For Maybaum, the Holocaust is an example of a so-called *churban* event, which through its destruction has helped human advancement through the medium of spiritual development. He maintains that in Auschwitz, the Jews suffered vicarious atonement for the sins of mankind, and with its passing comes the world's movement from medievalism to modernity. For Maybaum, the after-Auschwitz experience has allowed Jews to engage freely in all of the possibilities open to them through enlightenment and political emancipation.

IN SUMMATION

This brief survey of positions related to Holocaust theology has shown how different people have seen the events of Nazi persecution from a different perspective. Each of these responses can at best be partial descriptions and solutions to the quantity of evil witnessed during the Holocaust. Is it likely that many future Jewish thinkers will continue to wrestle and grapple with the theological responses to the Holocaust, producing an ever rich and diversified literature to add to the ranks of that which already exists.

11

Explaining God: Theology for Younger Children

Parents usually do not know how to answer their children's questions about God. Perhaps it is because they themselves do not talk or think about God very much in their own personal lives, or perhaps they lack a personal knowledge of what Judaism has to say about God and have not had a chance to develop their own personal theology. Whatever be the case, parents cannot really escape confronting the issue of God with their children, since children often wonder about God and ask questions about God in ways that reveal a great deal about their world views and their own conceptual development.

In the earlier chapters of this book, we have seen the many different ways in which God has been portrayed and spoken. There is no single, definitive, authoritative Jewish concept of God that has universal agreement. Exposing children to the variety of Jewish theological possibilities will help them eventually to determine their own spiritual model.

Rabbi Daniel Syme, in an essay entitled *Talking to Kids About God,* offers several guidelines for parents when attempting to talk to their children about God:

1. Do not offer the biblical notion of God—or any one concept—as "the" Jewish God idea.
2. When you speak to your children about God, state your personal beliefs, but clearly indicate that they are your beliefs.
3. Use appropriate language when discussing God with children of younger ages.
4. When your child volunteers a personal notion as to the nature of God, try to tie that affirmation to a great Jewish thinker.
5. Never be embarrassed to respond "I don't know" to a child's question about God.
6. Do not hesitate to consult with your rabbi, Jewish educator, or others to deal with difficult questions.
7. Encourage your children to share their thoughts about God and instances when they feel they have experienced God in their lives.
8. Listen better.
9. Emphasize to your children that our personal ideas of God grow as we grow, both in depth and in complexity.
10. Help your child see ritual, prayer, and holiday observances as ways in which the Jewish people express their attachment to God.
11. Do not be reluctant to share stories of times in your life when you experienced or felt close to God.

The following are ten questions and suggested answers to typical questions that are asked about God by children. Feel free to use and adapt them in any way you see fit.

1. Is there really a God in the world? God means many different things to many different people. The Bible portrays God as the creator of the world, a God who cares for people and acts in history. One of God's greatest acts, according to the Bible, was helping to free the Jewish people from Egyptian slavery.

While it is impossible to prove that any of the things written about God are absolutely true, there clearly seems to be evidence that there is a God if you take a very close look at the things all around you. For example, when you see a seed grow into a flower or a tree, or a beautiful sunrise or sunset, or a lovely waterfall, or other splendid things in nature, this has led many people to know that God is real. Only God could have made things like these in nature.

For other people, when they see an act of kindness and goodness, they become struck with the fact that to be a human being means much more than simply to live physically in the world. Here again, they may feel the existence of God.

The older you get, and the more closely you pay attention to the world, its design, and its order, you will come to feel closer to God and realize that everything in it is part of God's great plan.

2. Who created God? This question is often asked by a young child who has come to realize that all created things have a creator. Here is a suggested answer:

The God of the world is unique and totally different than anything else in the entire universe. God is One, the only one, and existed before there was a world. God has no mother and father, and is not like a human being. God has no beginning or end or birth because God has always existed. God is the one creator of everything in the world, always there, the one who started all of life.

3. Where does God live? In Jewish tradition, God has had many living spaces. For example, when the people of Israel wandered through the desert for forty years during biblical times, Moses built the tabernacle as a place of prayer. Years later, King Solomon built the magnificent Temple in Jerusalem, and there people came to speak to God through prayer and sacrifice.

After the Jerusalem Temples were destroyed, synagogues began to emerge. To this day, these houses of prayer are where people come to pray to God.

All of these special places that have been constructed as houses of prayer are not the only places where God dwells. In fact, Jewish tradition teaches that God lives everywhere in the universe, including in our synagogues, in nature, in our homes, and in people too.

In a very famous Hassidic story, the same question—where does God live—was asked. This was the question with which the Rabbi of Kotzk surprised a number of learned men who happened to be visiting him. They laughed at him: "What a stupid thing to ask! Is not the whole world full of his glory!" Then he answered his own question: "God dwells wherever people let him in."

God is everywhere and lives everywhere. You can find Him where you look for Him.

4. Does God speak to people? In the Bible, God frequently talks to people, including the likes of Noah,

Abraham, Moses, and all of the Jewish prophets. We are not exactly sure, though, the exact manner in which God was able to communicate. And so people have asked: Did the people hear actual words of God, much like human speech? We really will never know the answer to this question. The one thing we do know, though, is that people "heard" God's voice and instructions and acted upon them.

The great prophets and poets of Israel saw and heard God everywhere: "The voice of the Lord is upon the water. The voice of the Lord breaks cedars. The voice of the Lord hews out flames of fire" (Psalm 29).

People who listen carefully can hear God speak, even today. There are people who come to the synagogue not only to pray words to God, but to listen to God speak to them. Every time a Jewish person performs a *mitzvah,* one of God's commandments, he or she is in a sense hearing God speak to him or her.

So keep listening carefully. The more carefully you do so, the more likely you will get to hear God.

5. Is there evidence that God does answer prayers? Talking to God is praying, and the things we say to God are called our prayers. Some of your prayers are likely prayers that ask God for things. You may want a new toy, so you ask God for one in your prayers. God does hear you, but if you get a toy, the toy is not coming from God, but rather from the person who bought it for you.

Sometimes we pray for people who are sick to get well. This is a less selfish prayer than praying for a new toy, and hopefully the person who is sick will get well, although he or she may not. But be assured that God hears this prayer, too, even though we will never be able to understand fully how God answers prayers.

Sometimes we pray to God to thank God for some good thing that we have received. This is a very important kind of prayer, for it not only shows God our appreciation of Him, but also reminds us of the good thing that we have been given.

Prayer is, for Jewish people, often a way of reminding them to look inside of themselves and evaluate those things in their lives that are good and for which they need to show appreciation, and those things they need to improve. It's important for you to remember to keep praying regularly, for the more you do so, the more you will solidify your relationship with God, and the more comfortable you will be and feel in communicating with Him. And yes, God can and does hear and listen to your prayers!

Some say that the most important letter in the whole Torah is the *alef,* the first Hebrew letter of the Ten Commandments and the first letter of the Hebrew word for God. *Alef* is a silent letter, and one famous mystical story says that the entire Torah is contained in this silent letter. Listen carefully, and you too will be able to hear it.

6. *If God is supposedly all-good and all-powerful, why are there bad things in the world?* The first answer is that since we are not God, we will never be able to know why God seems to allow bad things to happen in the world.

Most of the bad things in the world come from people who choose to do bad things. They make bad choices and bad decisions. For instance, when a person kills another person, this is not God's doing. We know this because back in biblical times, one of God's Ten Commandments was "do not kill." Similarly, we know too that when a person steals from another person, this too is not what God wants, because God also said "do not steal."

God is a good God, and God is very powerful as well. We believe that God created the world, and with the creation of the world came the possibility of disease, floods, hurricanes, earthquakes, and people who do bad things. With God's act of creation, God gave mother nature freedom to act. God also gave to all people freedom to choose what they want to do, and unfortunately, some people make the wrong decisions and choose to hurt or cause damage to things and people in the world.

There is much more good than bad in the world. The bad, however, gets more of the publicity. Since God wanted us to be His servants, it is important for us to do our best helping God to make the world a better place for all to live. The more good we do and can influence others to do good, the better the world will be.

7. *If God is not a person, why do we call God words like "King" and "Father" in our prayers?* It is true that God is not a person. In fact, we believe that God is invisible and we can't see God, because God is not a thing, nor does God have any shape.

When we pray to God, we need to be able to call God by name or to describe characteristics that God has. For example, in most of the blessings that we recite as part of our prayers, we call God *melekh ha'olam*—King of the Universe. Now if God is not a person, then you might ask: How can God be a king, who is a person?

What you need to remember is that the people who wrote these prayers needed to help the people who pray be able to "visualize" God and think about some of His characteristics. After all, it's difficult to pray to a Being that is invisible. And so, when God is called a king in the prayer book, it does not mean that God is really a king, but rather that there are things that we can say about God that are similar to a king. For example, just as a king is powerful, mighty, and commands respect, so too is God. Just as a king has subjects who obey his laws, so too does God have people such as us, who are His subjects and who obey His laws. Similarly, when God is sometimes called an *avinu*—our Father, it does not literally mean that God is a father. Rather, it is the prayer book's way of saying that God can be like our parent—a father, who is tender, loving, and caring.

Always remember that everything that is written or said about God is the way humans attempt to describe Him figuratively. In this way, we are helped to understand better a God that we cannot see.

8. Is it permissible ever to get angry with God? Getting angry is part and parcel of life itself. People often get angry when they are frustrated or when something does not go the way in which they wanted it. Anger is often a way of letting out our feelings. With time and a little help from our friends and loved ones, the anger will usually go away.

There may come a time in your life when you feel that God has let you down. It's okay to get angry with God, especially if you have developed a close relationship to Him by always letting Him know what is on your mind. People often express their anger to God when they feel that God, the always dependable One, has not helped them when they needed God's help. Such people feel hurt, which causes them to become frustrated and very angry, often blaming God. Hopefully when this happens, you will have friends and family who will help to comfort and support you. God, too, has been known to comfort, help, and support people in their time of difficulty. Try to remember always that God is probably not the cause of what has happened to you that has caused you to be angry. It is more likely that God is on your side, waiting for you to ask for His help. Keep waking up every day and thanking God for all of those good things in your life. This will forever strengthen your relationship with God and allow you to challenge Him in your time of need.

9. Are there such things as miracles? Did God really part the Red Sea? Most people in the past accepted the miracles of the Bible, including one of the greatest when the waters of the Red Sea parted allowing the Israelites to escape from the Egyptians. Nothing in our religion discourages such belief, for nothing is impossible for a God who is all-powerful. There are other people who have spent a lot of time in order to find natural explanations for the miracles in the Bible. Thus, for example, they might believe that the dividing of the Red Sea developed as a result of low tides and sudden high winds, or the walls of Jericho tumbled because of an earthquake.

You are free to understand these and other miraculous events any way in which you so desire. The one thing that we know for certain is that the Jewish people against the greatest of all odds were freed from Egypt and that something spectacular did happen as they made their great escape.

Miracles also continue to occur today. Every time a person recovers from a life-threatening illness or when a new cure is discovered for a dreaded disease, it is, in a sense, one of the mysteries and wonders of life. It is important to continue to look for the everyday great wonders in the world. Whether it be a shooting star, or a magnificent waterfall, an eclipse of the moon, or an awesome bolt of lightning, each of these is evidence of that awesome and wondrous power that we call God.

10. Did God really play favorites and choose the Jews to be His special people? The idea that the Jewish people were specially selected by God to carry out God's special purposes is prominent in the Bible and in other Jewish teachings, too. For example, the Book of Exodus (19:4–6) states the following: "If you will listen to Me and keep My covenant, then you shall be My own treasure from all peoples . . . And you shall be a holy nation."

In the Book of Deuteronomy, we learn that God chose the Jewish people because He loved them.

In the Books of the Prophets, the idea of the chosen people is further refined. For example, in the Book of Isaiah (42:6–7) we learn the following: "I am God, I have called you in righteousness. . . . I have given you a covenant for the people. For a light to the nations, to open the eyes of the blind."

To return to the original question regarding whether God plays favorites with the Jews and did God actually choose the Jewish people to the exclusion of others, no one really knows for sure. It certainly seems unlikely.

What is important is that the Jewish people believed that God had chosen them and given them a mission to be a holy people. Israel's mission that went hand in hand with its being chosen by God was to be a light to all of the nations, and to help bring more righteousness and justice into the world.

For many observant Jews, it means accepting God's commandments *(mitzvot)* and carefully following them and living by them, thus dedicating their lives to God.

12

DOING YOUR OWN THEOLOGY

One very great difficulty for people who wish to make prayer a part of their lives is their personal concern about God and God's nature. Some are unsure of their beliefs because they have never had an opportunity to do some serious thinking about them and formulate their personal God ideas. Others feel that since they doubt or may not even believe in God, involving themselves in a prayer experience would be hypocritical.

The Jewish people have questioned God since biblical times, sometimes even challenging God on a decision that He made. Who can forget Abraham's great challenge to God's justice when he learns that God will destroy all the inhabitants of Sodom and Gomorrah for their wickedness: "Shall not the Judge of all the earth do justly?" For Abraham, an unjust God would be a contradiction in terms. We have seen the variety of thoughts and ideas related to God by Jewish theologians throughout our history, leading to the conclusion that there is no single authoritative Jewish theology to which all subscribe.

The purpose of this chapter is to provide the reader with a more systematic context in which to develop his or her own personal theology and God beliefs. Although you can work on your own on these exercises and questions, you may find it beneficial to work with another person or within a study group. Group learning allows for a sharing of thoughts and views, and often helps to stimulate the discussion.

EXERCISE 1: QUESTIONS ABOUT GOD

In this exercise, you will find a series of questions related to how you envision God and God's powers. Try to answer the following questions as openly and honestly as possible.

1. How do you communicate with God? When do you feel you have been the most successful?
2. Have you ever felt God's Presence? What were the circumstances?
3. Do you find meaning in saying prayers to God? Do you feel that praying to God has helped you in any way?
4. Do you ever take time to thank God for good things in your life? What were the times you did this?
5. Have you ever been angry with God? Describe such a time.
6. What are some ways of making God's Name holy?
7. Do you have any proof(s) that God really exists?

8. Do you think God spoke real words to the Jewish prophets many years ago? Has God ever spoken to you? If so, what was said?

9. Do you think that God needs people in order truly to exist?

10. Do you think that there are certain places in the world where God can be especially found more than others? Which are they?

11. Do you think that God loves all people in the world? Are there some people that God loves more than others?

12. In the covenants between God and Abraham and God and Moses, do you think that the Jewish people have kept their part?

13. Do you have any special gifts that you believe God needs?

14. What might cause some people to doubt the existence of God?

15. Which is easier, believing in God or not believing in God? Explain.

16. What is the importance to you of the Jewish belief in one God?

17. Does your relationship with God mean that you have special responsibilities in the world? If so, what are they?

18. How do you think people came to know that there was a God in the world?

19. What do you think is the purpose of life on this earth? How does your answer relate to God's existence?

20. Do you think that people can train themselves to hear God?

21. In what way(s) can a person imitate God?
22. If you were God, what would you do differently?

EXERCISE 2: STATEMENTS OF WHAT YOU
BELIEVE ABOUT GOD

Some nine hundred years ago, the famous philosopher Maimonides wrote one of the most well known creeds of Jewish Faith. It has come to be known as the Thirteen Principles of Jewish Faith, and includes such statements as: I believe that God is One, I believe that God is the Creator of all things, I believe that God is incorporeal, I believe that God is the first and the last, I believe that there will never be another Torah given by God, I believe that God knows all of a person's thoughts, and so forth. In establishing his thirteen faith principles, Maimonides in reality was saying that being Jewish itself is an obligation. In doing so, the myth of often repeated expressions such as "I am a Jew at heart" is put to rest. Rather than a "do your own thing" system defined by each individual, being Jewish to Maimonides means articulation of his established thirteen principles of faith.

A hundred years after the death of Maimonides, Rabbi Daniel bar Yehudah of Rome made the thirteen principles into a song, known as the *Yigdal*. It is included in most prayer books and sung in synagogues around the world.

Here are some questions and points for discussion about God based on Maimonides' Thirteen Principles of Faith. Try to answer and discuss as many as you can.

1. I believe that God is the Creator and Ruler of all things.

   Yes _____

   No _____

   i. What does it mean that God is both a Creator and Ruler? Do you think it is possible that God could be one of these without the other?

   ii. If you believe that God created the world, why do you think that He did so?

   iii. Do you believe that God gets involved in human affairs and in things that He created? Do you have any evidence to support this?

2. I believe that God is One and that there is no unity that is in any way like His. He alone is our God— He was, He is, and He will be.

   Yes _____

   No _____

   i. What does it mean to you that God's unity is unlike any other?

   ii. Would you describe God as being simple? If so, can you imagine anything as simple as God?

   iii. Do you believe that God can exist in space? Can the concept of position apply to Him?

   iv. Do you believe in a God that is eternal?

3. I believe that God does not have a body. Physical concepts do not apply to Him. There is nothing whatsoever that resembles Him at all.

   Yes _____

   No _____

     i. If God has no body, what do you think the Torah means when it says that man was created in "the image of God" (Genesis 1:26)?

    ii. What nonphysical things in the world affect your life? Do any of these nonphysical things resemble God?

   iii. If God has no image or body, why is the Bible filled with references to attributes of God, such as God's right hand, nostrils, face, and so forth?

4. I believe that God is the first and that God is the last.

Yes _____

No _____

     i. What do you think existed before God?

    ii. Children often ask, "Who created God?" Discuss this question.

   iii. What does the principle of "God is the last" mean to you?

   iv. Why does Maimonides consider time as something that was created?

5. I believe that it is only proper to pray to God. One may not pray to anyone or anything else.

Yes _____

No _____

     i. Why do you think that idolatry and belief in many gods are forbidden in Judaism?

    ii. An earthly king often depends on his subordinates to help him rule. Do you think that this is ever true of God, who is sometimes called the King? How does this relate to this principle?

    iii. Do you think that God can answer prayer?

    iv. If you think that God cannot answer prayer, are there any other reasons or benefits to saying prayers? Explain your answer.

6. I believe that the entire Torah that we now have is that which was given to Moses.

Yes _____

No _____

    i. What do you believe the role of Moses was in writing the Torah?

    ii. Do you believe that Moses was the sole writer of the Torah?

    iii. What do you think people in the Bible heard when God spoke to them?

    iv. Do you believe that God still speaks to people today? Has God ever spoken to you? Explain.

7. I believe that the Torah will not be changed and that there will never be another Torah given by God.

Yes _____

No _____

    i. Do you think that there are laws in the Torah that are no longer applicable to today's society? If so, what are they, and why are they no longer applicable?

    ii. Do you believe that God knows what will happen in the future? If so, why do you think that God did not create a Torah with laws and customs that would be applicable for all time to come?

    iii. Do you think that anything in the Torah can and will ever become "old fashioned"?

    iv. Do you think that the entire Torah is the
        word of God? If not, what, in your opinion,
        are the other possibilities?

8. I believe that God knows all of man's deeds and
    thoughts.

    Yes _____

    No _____

    i. If God knows what we will do in the future,
      how are we still given freedom of choice?

    ii. In what way do you believe that God could
       know the future?

9. I believe that God rewards those who keep His
    commandments and punishes those who trans-
    gress His commandments.

    Yes _____

    No _____

    i. When you follow a God-given command-
      ment, do you do so because God commanded
      you?

    ii. Why do good people sometimes suffer and
       evil people prosper? How does this fit with
       this principle of faith?

    iii. Who decides what is good and what is evil?
        How do you know what is right in the world
        and what is wrong?

    iv. Do you think that God is aware of what you
       do? If so, does this influence your behavior
       and things you do in life?

10. I believe that the dead will be brought back to
    life when God wills it to happen.

    Yes _____

    No _____

    i. Exactly what do you think resurrection of the dead means?

   ii. Ezekiel, chapter 37, describes a vision where bones in a valley grow skin and come back to life. Do you believe that this vision really happened? If so, how do you explain it?

  iii. Do you believe in the immortality of a person's soul?

  iv. Do you believe in heaven or hell?

   v. Do you believe in the possibility of reincarnation?

EXERCISE 3: NAMES OF GOD

As previously stated in an earlier chapter, God has a variety of names that have been given to Him in the Bible, rabbinic literature, and in the prayer book. Each name often reflects a particular attribute about God or characteristic that is part of God's so-called essence. Here is a partial listing of God's names. Find a quiet place and read this list with a friend or people in your study group. Share your preferences, and talk about how it feels when you address God using a variety of different names.

1. *Adonai.*
2. *Elohim.*
3. *Shaddai,* Almighty One.
4. *Adonai Tzeva'ot.*
5. Rock.
6. Rock of Ages.
7. *Kadosh* (Holy One).
8. *Shalom* (Peace).

9. Shield of Abraham.
10. *El Adon.*
11. Our Shepherd.
12. Our Father.
13. Our King.
14. King of Kings.
15. I am that I am.
16. *HaShem* (The Name).
17. The Infinite One.
18. Shechinah.
19. The Eternal One.
20. Master of the Universe.
21. Redeemer.
22. *HaMakom* (The Place).
23. The Healer.
24. The Compassionate One.
25. Judge of the Earth.
26. Mighty One.
27. God of Jacob.
28. *Shaddai* (Almighty).
29. The Guide.
30. Hidden of Hiddens.
31. Ancient of Ancients.
32. Living God.
33. Bountiful One.
34. *Yah.*
35. The Judge.

EXERCISE 4: TWENTY SENTENCE COMPLETIONS

1. I most need God when _____.
2. I feel closest to God when _____.

3. I am most likely to pray to God when _____.
4. I like to thank God when _____.
5. I have struggled with God when _____.
6. I sometimes doubt God when _____.
7. I believe in God when _____.
8. I have seen God perform miracles when _____.
9. I wonder about God when _____.
10. People most need God when _____.
11. God most needs people when _____.
12. I most feel like a chosen person of God when __.
13. To believe in God means _____.
14. Not to believe in God means _____.
15. My belief about God is _____.
16. For me, God is _____.
17. God's most important attribute is _____.
18. I feel God's love when _____.
19. I most feel God's anger when _____.
20. I am most likely to call God when _____.

EXERCISE 5: POSITION PAPER ON REVELATION

Write a personal statement about what you think happened at Mount Sinai when God spoke to the Israelites.

EXERCISE 6: FINDING GOD IN THE WORLD

Write several paragraphs on how you have found or think you can find God in the world.

EXERCISE 7: FINDING GOD IN YOUR RELIGION

How can your religion help you to find God? Write about it.

EXERCISE 8: GOD'S COMMANDMENTS

Which of God's commandments are most important to you personally? Which are you most likely to observe, and why are you most likely to observe these and not others?

EXERCISE 9: THE CHOSEN PEOPLE OF GOD

In what sense do you believe that the Jewish people were chosen by God?

EXERCISE 10: GOD AND THE BIBLE

What role do you think God played in writing the Bible?

EXERCISE 11: GOD AND PRAYER

There are various reasons why people pray, some personal and some communal. When you find yourself praying, what are your reasons for doing so? Where does God fit into the picture?

EXERCISE 12: WONDER STATEMENTS

Fill in the blanks.

1. I wonder if God _____
2. I wonder why God _____
3. I wonder whether God _____
4. I wonder when God _____

EXERCISE 13: WRITE A THEOLOGICAL WILL

A most beautiful Jewish custom that is not well known in our time is the writing of an ethical will. Parents and grandparents would write letters to their children and grandchildren expressing their hopes for the future and the values they bequeathed to their descendants. Today there is a renewed interest in writing such ethical wills. In Judaism, ethics is an extension of theology. Try to write an ethical will, including in it a statement related to your own personal theology.

13

NOTABLE QUOTATIONS AND PASSAGES ABOUT GOD

The following is a compendium of important passages in talmudic, midrashic, and philosophical literature that are intended to shed light on the way in which God has been perceived throughout Jewish history. The passages are listed by category, which helps to define broadly their area of concern.

PETITIONING TO GOD

In the following passages, we see examples of people petitioning God. In them, we learn several principles related to petitioning, including the rabbinic quotes that prayer must not become a fixed task, but rather a plea to God for grace and mercy. We also learn that God can and often does answer the petitions of people.

1. God, you must redeem us eventually. Why delay? *(Midrash Tehillim).*

2. God, I have done my part. Now You do Yours *(Shemot Rabbah* 23:8).

3. If tribulation befalls a person, let that person not cry out to Michael or Gabriel, but only to God (Jerusalem Talmud *Berakhot* 9:1).

4. A Child's Prayer: Rabbi Elezar and his companions heard of the serious illness of Rabbi Jose at Pekiin. When they met with the people of the town, they learned that he was near death. In the home of the sick man they saw a young child embracing its father and crying bitterly. Then the little boy prayed: "You have written in Your Torah, O God, that the children may be taken away and the mother must be spared. My father was to me and my younger sister, both father and mother, since my mother died. And now You are taking him from us as well. It were better You did take us to You and leave him on earth, in agreement with Your law."

The Rabbis had not heart to remain and listen, and went into another room. When the boy had fallen asleep in utter exhaustion, they took him to his own bed, and again entered the room of the stricken Rabbi. And lo, he opened his eyes and greeted them. They awoke the child and brought him in to see that his prayer for his father had been heard.

The Rabbis went on their way, and since the day was very hot, they entered a cave. There they found a dead robber, with a purse of gold tied around his belt. They took the belt with the purse and remained for a moment to see what would happen. Soon there came a man, and not observing the Rabbis, he prayed thus: "You know, God, that I do not bewail for myself the loss of my money which the robber has taken from me. But I have aged parents to sustain. Moreover, some of the money belonged to a poor man who had saved it for his daughter's dowry." The Rabbis gave him the purse (*Zohar* III:204).

5. Rabbi Jacob in the name of Rabbi Eliezer said: "And that you do not hide yourself from your own flesh?" (Isaiah 58:7). This means: "From your own divorced wife." In the days of Rabbi Tanchuma, Israel was in dire need of rain. The people implored the rabbi to proclaim a fast day. He did so, once, twice, and yet no rain came. The third time he commanded that everyone find a poor person and give him charity. A man went to do so and was approached by his divorced wife. She said to him: "Gain merit through me, for since I have left you, I have seen no single good day." He took pity on her and gave her the money. An eyewitness informed the rabbi, saying: "If this man did not mean to offend with his divorced wife, he would not have given her money." The rabbi summoned the man and received his explanation. The rabbi thereupon declared: "This man had good cause to refuse pity to this woman, and he was not supposed to support her. Yet he was filled with compassion for her. We, O God, the Children of Your beloved Abraham, Isaac, and Jacob, are dependent only upon You for our support in life. Since You are the All Compassionate, should You not succor us and send us rain?"

At once the world was relieved, and the drought ended (*Leviticus Rabbah,* 34).

6. Rabbi Simeon ben Nathaniel said: Do not make your prayer a fixed task, but a plea to God for grace and mercy (*Ethics of the Fathers,* 2, 18).

7. Israel says to God: " 'Be like a deer or a young hart' (Song of Songs 8:14). As a deer sleeps with one eye

open and one eye closed You be like this with regard to us" (*Zohar* II:14).

BLESSINGS AND GRACE OF GOD

In these passages, we see the importance of praising God for all that God has does for humanity. It is also equally important to praise God with a joyous heart, and even to praise God when things occur that are not happy events. This is illustrated in the traditional blessing that one says when learning of the loss of a loved one: "Blessed are You, O God, You are the true Judge." This prayer is a reaffirmation of a mourner's faith in God and in the worthwhileness of life, even during a time of great sorrow. It also recognizes God as the final judge of all humankind.

1. First bless God and then bless others (*Zohar* I:227b).

2. It is proper for a person to praise God for every breath he takes (*Genesis Rabbah* 14:9).

3. The person who receives enjoyment in this world without blessing God for it, robs both God and the community of Israel (*Zohar* III:44b).

4. The person who alters the wording of the Sages in benedictions has not fulfilled his duty (Talmud *Berakhot* 40).

5. Everything that breathes shall praise God; this also means: for every breath a person breathes, it is that person's duty to praise his Maker (*Deuteronomy Rabbah* 2, 37).

6. All whom God created in His world, praise Him and sing to Him (*Zohar* I:123a).

7. A Rabbi asked: "Why do we recite every day the Eighteen Benedictions?"

Rabbi Samuel ben Nachman replied: "Because eighteen times are the patriarchs mentioned jointly in the Torah. The first joint mention is in the words: 'But God will surely remember you, and bring you out of this land to the land which God swore to Abraham, to Isaac and to Jacob' " (*Tanchuma, Vayera* sec. 1).

8. The person who blesses God is likewise blessed (*Zohar* I:250a).

9. Say the Grace after the meal in a spirit of joy. If you bless God with joy, God will bless you with joy and plenty (*Zohar* II:218a).

10. It is a person's duty to bless God for the untoward events of life by saying: "Blessed be the faithful Judge," just as He blesses God for the good (*Mishnah Berakhot* 9:5).

11. Offering God encouragement: Rabbi Joshua ben Levi said: When Moses ascended on High, he found God making ornaments for the letters. God said to him: "There comes no greeting from you?" Moses answered: "May a serf, then, greet his Master?"

God answered: "But you may encourage Me." Moses responded at once: "And now, I pray You, let the power of God be great" (Numbers 14:17) (Talmud *Shabbat* 29).

12. Rabbi Simeon ben Yochai says: "You are My witnesses, says the Lord, and I am God" (Isaiah 43:10). When you are My witnesses, I am God, and when you are not My witnesses, I am not your God (*Sifre* Deuteronomy, par. 346; *Pesikta Buber* 102b).

13. "When Israel is of one counsel on earth, God's great Name is praised in Heaven." Rabbi Simeon ben

Yochai illustrates this by the figure of a palace built on two boats lashed together, and the consequence if the boats are separated. Similarly he continues: " 'This is my God, and I will make Him lovely' (Exodus 15:2). When I praise Him, He is lovely, and when I do not praise Him, He is, so to speak, lovely in Himself . . . Again, when, 'Unto You do I lift my eyes, O You that sits in the Heavens' (Psalm 123:1). Otherwise, it were as if He should not be sitting in the Heavens'' (Talmud *Shabbat* 133b; *Mechilta Shirah* 3).

14. Disparaging God: A person ascended the pulpit of the Precentor in the presence of Rabbi Hanina. He recited the words: "The Great, Mighty, Awesome, Exalted, Brave, Strong, True, Fearful, Powerful God." The Rabbi waited until the man had finished, and then said to him: "Have you completed the praises of your maker? As for the first three adjectives, if Moses had not included them in the Torah (Deuteronomy 10:17), and the Men of the Great Assembly in the Amidah, we should not have said them. Yet you say so many. It is like a king who possesses millions of gold pieces, and someone praises him as the possessor of millions of silver pieces. Would this not be a derogation of him?" (Talmud *Berakhot* 33).

15. Excess in recounting the praises of God is explicitly forbidden, for it is written: "Who can utter the mighty acts of God, or proclaim all of God's praise?" (Talmud *Megillah* 18a; Psalm 106:2).

16. God wants man's blessing: Rabbi Ishmael ben Elisha, the High Priest, said: "I went into the Holy of Holies to offer incense, and I saw the Crowned God of Hosts seated on His Throne. He said to me: 'Ishmael,

My son, bless Me.' I responded: 'God of the Universe, may it be Your Will that Your mercies subdue Your anger, and that Your mercies be revealed in Your attributes, and that You conduct Yourself with Your sons in the attribute of mercy; and that You judge them not according to the strict letter of justice.' And God bowed His head to me. This should teach us that the blessing of an unimportant person not be light in our eyes.'' (Talmud *Berakhot* 7).

17.   The value of a blessing: One man performed a *mitzvah* but a second man recited the benediction. Rabban Gamliel decreed that the second man pay the first ten guldens for taking away the benediction. It was asked: Is it the *mitzvah* or the benediction that is worth ten guldens, inasmuch as the Grace after Meals contains four benedictions, but is a single *mitzvah?*

The answer is found in the following story. A Sadducee came to Rabbi and said: ''We read in Amos (4:13): 'For lo, He that forms the mountains and creates the wind.' Since of one thing it is said that it was formed, and of the other, that it was created, it appears that there are two makers, one who creates and another who forms.'' Rabbi said: ''Look to the end of the verse: 'The Lord, the God of Hosts, is His Name.' He is Only One.'' The Sadducee promised to return in three days with a proper rejoinder. On the third day Rabbi's servant announced that a Sadducee wished to enter. Rabbi was reluctant to continue the argument, but since the man was of a prominent family, he consented to see him. The man entered and said: ''I came to bring these tidings: your opponent found no report, and fell from a roof and died.'' Rabbi invited him to dinner, after which he said to him: "By reason of your tidings, you can choose between the recitation of the Grace after Meals with the glass of wine accompanying it, or the receipt of forty guldens." The man chose the Grace and the Cup of Blessing. Later he received a peerage in Rome. From this you may learn that each benediction is worth ten guldens (Talmud *Chullin* 87).

18. Praise for five attributes: The words "Bless God, O my soul" (Psalm 103:104) were said five times by David with reference both to God and the soul. As God fills the whole world, so does the soul fill the whole body; as God sees and is not seen, so with the soul; as God nourishes the whole world, so does the soul nourish the whole body; as God is pure, so also is the soul pure; as God dwells in secret, so does the soul. Therefore let him who possesses these five properties praise God to whom these five attributes belong (Talmud *Berakhot* 10a).

GOD AS OUR CARETAKER

The image of God as the Caretaker and Guardian of people is evident from the following passages. What is especially notable is God's constant concern for the poor and lowly.

1. He who brings forth a generation clothes it (Jerusalem Talmud *Kilaim* 9:4).

2. A man may cleave to a rich man, as long as he is rich. But when the rich man becomes poor, he is ridiculed. But God cleaves to the poor (Jerusalem Talmud *Berakhot* 9:1).

3. God does evil to no person, but when God turns His gaze away from a person, that person thereby goes to ruin (*Zohar* I; *Midrash ha-Neelam* 115a).

4. A high placed person cares to attend to others only if they are of the same rank. But God attends to the lowly *(Sotah)*.

5. God created and God provides. God made and God sustains (*Tanchuma, Buber, Vayera,* par. 24).

6. God's watchful eye: Rabbi Simeon ben Yohai and his disciples, while walking, came upon a stream with no bridge to cross it. Rabbi Jose complained: "What need was there to place a stream in this deserted place?"

Rabbi Simeon answered: "Such a complaint is sinful. Everything here exists for a purpose and the Creator has found everything to be good." As he spoke, a snake coiled swiftly between their feet. "Be not alarmed," said the Master. "It may be vouchsafed to us to receive confirmation of the truth of my words." They then beheld the snake engaged in a battle with a viper, and eventually both fell over dead. "Had not God sent the snake," said the Master, "the viper might have wounded us" *(Zohar; Emor).*

7. Rabbi Joseph said: Two men were about to embark upon a mercantile enterprise; one of them, having had a thorn pierce his foot, was compelled to forego his intended journey and bemoaned his lot. Later he learned that the ship in which his companion had sailed, had sunk at sea. He confessed his shortsightedness, and praised God in the words of Isaiah (20:1): "I will praise You, O God, because You were

angry with me. Your anger will depart and You will comfort me" (Talmud *Niddah* 31a).

GOD'S COMPASSION FOR WICKED PEOPLE

In the following passages, we learn that one of God's important attributes is that of grace and mercy. God gives His grace (i.e., undeserved merit) to even the wicked of the earth. The implication seems to be that God provides a second chance for wicked people, allowing them the possibility of repentance and changing their ways.

1. In what is God's strength demonstrated? In His patience with the wicked? (Talmud *Yoma* 69).

2. When the Egyptians were drowning, the angels wished to sing. But God said: "My handiwork is dying, and you wish to sing?" (Talmud *Megillah* 10).

3. Even the evil which God brings down upon the world, God brings down with wisdom (Jerusalem Talmud *Yevamot* 8:3).

4. Man is not immediately punished for his evil life. God has more patience with men of evil than with the just (*Zohar* I:140a).

5. "God upholds all that fall, and raises up those that are bowed down" (Psalm 145:14). It does not say: "Those that stand" but "those that are bowed down"—even the wicked (*Tanchuma, Buber, Vayetze,* par. 10).

6. When Moses ascended on High, he saw God writing the word: "Long-suffering." He said: "Are You, O God, long-suffering to the righteous?" God answered: "To the righteous and to the unrighteous."

Moses responded: "But the unrighteous, O God, deserve immediate punishment."

God replied: "You shall see that you will think differently at a later time."

When Israel sinned, God wished to punish them at once. But Moses said: "Not as I have said, do You, O God, but act as You say: 'And now, I pray You, let the power of God be great, according as You have spoken' " (Numbers 14:17) (Talmud *Sanhedrin* 111).

GOD AS THE PHYSICIAN

Described in the following passages are portrayals of God as the Physician who is able to cure those who are sick. In Jewish liturgy, God is sometimes called the *Rofeh*—the Healer.

1. God creates the cure before God sends the malady (*Zohar* I:196a).

2. When a physician cures, the illness may reappear. When God heals, it never returns (*Zohar* III:303b).

3. God heals with the same thing that He uses to strike *(Mechilta Beshallach)*.

4. God heals bitterness with bitter remedies *(Mechilta Beshallach)*.

5. When King Hezekiah in his mortal illness heard the announcement of Isaiah in the name of God that he was to die, he replied: "We have a family tradition from David, that even if a sharp sword is resting at a man's throat, he should not refrain from craving mercy." Thereupon he prayed and was granted fifteen more years of life (Isaiah 38:1–5). Rabbi Yochanan and Rabbi Eleazar quote in this connection: "Though He slay me,

yet will I trust in Him" (Job 13:15) (Talmud *Berakhot* 10a).

6. Heal us, O God, and we shall be healed. Help us and save us, for You are our glory. Grant perfect healing for all our afflictions (from the *Amidah* prayer of the daily liturgy).

HOW TO HONOR AND DENY GOD

The following passages describe behavior that according to the Rabbis displays both a path to honoring God as well as a path to denying God's very existence.

1. A philosopher asked Rabbi Reuben of Tiberias: "Who is the most hated of people?" The reply was: "The person who denies his God. A transgression of any one of the Ten Commandments means a denial of God. The person who respects God will not have idols, swear falsely in God's name, desecrate God's Sabbath wantonly, forbear from honoring his parents, steal, murder, commit adultery or covet another's property" (*Tosefta Shavuot* 3:5).

2. The person who walks straight paths honors God (*Numbers Rabbah* 8:3).

3. Elijah said: "The person who increases the honor of God and diminishes his own honor shall see God's honor and his own increased" (*Numbers Rabbah* 4:21).

4. It was Abraham who first brought God down from the heavens to the earth, calling Him the God of the heavens and the God of the earth (*Sifre, Ha'azinu* 134b).

FAITH IN GOD

The passages below describe the importance of a person having faith and trust in God.

1. Rabbi Zeira said: "I was privileged to know a man with perfect trust in God. He set aside hours for the study of the Torah and no matter how much he stood to lose, he would never desist from his period of study. He would say: 'If God desires to send me profit, He can do so after my time of study' " (Talmud *Sotah* 9).

2. Said Rabbi Nehemiah: "Through faith alone Abraham our Father acquired this world and the World-to-Come, as it is written: 'And Abraham had faith in God' " (Genesis 15:16) (*Mechilta to Exodus* 14:31).

3. Rabbi Meir earned three selaim weekly. One he used for food, one for other necessities, and the third he donated to his school. His disciples inquired: "Why don't you save for your children?" He replied: "If they are righteous, God will provide for them; if unrighteous, why should I provide for those whom God dislikes?" (*Ecclesiastes Rabbah* 2).

4. God said to Moses: "The faith shown by the Children of Israel in obeying the command to march forward into the Red Sea is sufficient reason for Me to divide the sea for them" (*Mechilta Beshallach* 3).

5. Rabbi Eliezer the Great said: "The person who has a morsel of bread in his vessel and yet says, 'What shall I eat tomorrow?' is of those of little faith" (Talmud *Sotah* 48b).

6. The Israelites were delivered from Egypt only as a reward for faith, as it is written: "And the people believed" (Exodus 4:31) (*Mechilta Beshallach* 3).

7. One of the Sages said: "I am a child of God, and my neighbor is God's child too. My work is in the town, his in the fields. I rise early to my work, and he rises early to his. He boasts not of his work; I will not boast of mine. And if you say that I do great things, and he small things, I ask: 'Have we not learnt that it matters not whether a man accomplish much or little, if only he fix his heart upon his Father in Heaven?' " (Talmud *Berakhot* 17a).

8. "Why was Abraham so severely punished by God," asked the Rabbis, "that his children were to be enslaved in Egypt so many years?"

And they answered: "Because he showed a lack of faith in God's power, when after He assured him: 'I am God that brought you out of Ur of the Chaldees, to give to you this land, to inherit it,' Abraham said to God: 'How do I know that I shall inherit it?' " (Talmud *Nedarim* 32a).

GOD AS A PARENT

Many rabbinic passages refer to God as a parent, and compare God to both a mother and a father. Here are some examples of these passages.

1. There is no father except God (Talmud *Berakhot* 35a).

2. A son respects his father and a servant his master, but you, Israel, are ashamed to proclaim that I am your Father, or that you are My servants (*Zohar* I:103a).

3. God has compassion like a father, and comforts like a mother (*Pesikta Buber,* 139a).

4. Rabbi Judah ben Temah said: "Be strong as a leopard and swift as an eagle and fleet as a gazelle and brave

as a lion to do the will of Your Father Who is in Heaven''
(*Ethics of the Fathers* 5:23).

5. Rabbi Judah ben Ilai said: The fatherly care of God
for Israel is like a man walking on a journey whose son
precedes him; robbers came in front to take the boy
captive, but his father placed the lad behind him. A wolf
came from behind, but the father placed him in front. If
robbers came in front and wolves behind, the father
took his son in his arms. If the boy was troubled by the
heat of the sun, his father stretched his own garment
over him. If he became hungry, he gave him food;
thirsty, he gave him drink. Thus did God do on behalf of
Israel in the wilderness (*Mechilta Beshallach* 4).

6. Rabbi Phinehas said: A king left his country and
returned after an absence of several years. When he
arrived at his palace, his own sons did not recognize
him, but looked at each duke and count, searching their
faces in quest of their father. The King said: ''They are
without power; I am your father.'' Thus says God:
''Turn not unto the angels and saints. They are powerless to avail in your behalf. Turn to Me. I am your
Father'' (*Pesikta Rabbati* 21:11).

7. Our Father our King, we have sinned against You
(High Holiday liturgy).

GOD AS GIFTGIVER TO HUMANITY

There are rabbinic references related to gifts that God
has given to people. Here are several examples of God
as the Giftgiver.

1. Three fine gifts were given to the world: wisdom,
strength, and wealth (*Numbers Rabbah* 22:7).

2. Three fine gifts God gave to Israel: Torah, Palestine, and the World-to-Come. All are achieved only through chastisement (Talmud *Berakhot* 5).

3. When a person is beloved of God, God sends him poor men as gifts. If the man aids them, God then places upon him a thread of mercy, marking him as beyond the touch of the Angel of Punishment (*Zohar* I:104a).

4. A person who has obeyed one commandment is helped by Heaven to obey many commandments *(Mechilta Beshallach)*.

GOD AS GUARDIAN OF ISRAEL

Both in rabbinic literature and in Jewish liturgy, God has been portrayed as the Guardian of people. The Rabbis have interpreted one of the ancient names of God, *Shaddai*, as an acronym for the Hebrew words *Shomer Delatot Yisrael*—Guardian of Israelite Doors. The word *Shaddai* often appears on the front of the mezuzah receptacle, thus making the affixing of a mezuzah a way of ensuring God's watchfulness over a Jewish home. The following passages describe God as the Guardian of His people.

1. Rabbi Simeon ben Lakish taught the following parable concerning God's guardianship of Israel and God's association with Israel. A king fastened a chain to the key of a precious jewel box in his possession, lest it might be easily mislaid or lost. Even thus did God attach His name "El" to "Israel" to guard against their being lost among the nations of the world (Jerusalem Talmud, *Taanit* 11:6, 65d).

2. Hadrian said to Rabbi Joshua: "You are among us as a lamb among seventy wolves. Are we not to be commended for not consuming you?"

Rabbi Joshua replied: "It is not your goodness that saves us, but the fact that we have a great Shepherd as our guardian" *(Tanchuma to Toledot).*

3. The Lord is My Shepherd, and I shall not be lacking (Psalm 23:1).

4. Guardian of the people Israel, guard the remnant of Israel and let not Israel perish, those who say: *"Shema Yisrael"* (daily morning liturgy).

5. All who love God does God preserve, but all the wicked God destroys (Psalm 145:20, recited three times daily).

IMITATION OF GOD

Theologians often use the phrase *imitatio dei* to refer to the concept of imitating God. The concept has been generally said to be based on the verse *vehalachta bidrachav* (and you shall walk in God's ways). Rabbinic thinkers have explained this verse as a commandment that requires people to follow the attributes of God. For instance, as God clothed the first two humans (Adam and Eve), so too people should clothe the naked. The following verses relate to this fundamental theological concept.

1. Can a person go behind the Shechinah? The phrase means: Follow the example of the Shechinah. Imitate God (Talmud *Sotah* 14).

2. Abba Saul said: I will imitate God. As God is merciful and gracious, I will also be merciful and gracious (*Mechilta Shirah* 3).

3. We are the adherents of the King of Kings. What is the duty of the King's entourage? To imitate the king. (*Sifra* to Leviticus 19:2, "Be holy for I God am Holy.")

4. Walk in the ways of God. As God is merciful and gracious, so be you as well. As God is righteous and just, so be you as well. As God is Holy, so be you (*Sifre, Ekev* 85a).

5. Man is, in a sense, a creator, and therefore a collaborator with God (*Shabbat* 10a).

6. God, it is said, donned a *tallit* like a Reader of the congregation, and showed Moses the way of prayer, saying to him: "When the Israelites sin against Me, let them copy this example, and I will pardon their sins" (Talmud *Rosh Hashanah* 17b).

7. God is the great exemplar of lovingkindness. The world itself was created solely in lovingkindness (Psalm 89:3). Rabbi Simlai observes: The Pentateuch begins with an act of lovingkindness: God made garments of skin to clothe the man and his wife; and ends with another: He buried Moses in the valley. It is in such gracious deeds that man can and should imitate God, who clothes the naked, visits the sick, comforts the mourners, and buries the dead. (Talmud *Sotah* 14a; Talmud *Sukkah* 49b).

GOD AS JUDGE OF THE EARTH

Abraham, in a moment of extreme audacity, was one of the first to challenge God's justice. Unhappy with the fact that God was about to destroy all of Sodom and Gomorrah, Abraham asks, "Shall not the Judge of all

the earth do justly?'' (Genesis 18:25). Rabbinic literature is replete with references to God's heavenly tribunal, and the liturgy of both Rosh Hashanah and Yom
Kippur, also known as the Day of Judgment, is filled
with metaphors portraying God as the Judge on High,
weighing the sins of His people. The following are
sample quotations related to the theme of God's
judgment.

1. O God, You wish the world to exist, and You insist
upon true judgment (*Leviticus Rabbah* 10).

2. In the hour of judgment God says to man: ''Oh
man, much trouble have I taken with you before you
were born. Much trouble have I taken with you after
your birth. Have you, however, taken the trouble to
learn what you must do? Have you troubled to perform
in practice that which you have learned?''

If the person answers in the affirmative, God sets him
near to Him. If in the negative, God sends the man far
from Him. If the person is found to be good, his parents
enjoy a double reward in the World to Come: their own
reward and the contemplation of their son's reward. If
the man is found to be evil, his parents do not enjoy
even their own reward because of pity for their erring
son (*Mesikta Chibbut Hakever* 5).

3. Rabbi Simai said: ''It is written (Psalm 50:4): 'He
calls to the heavens above, and to the earth, that He may
judge His people.' 'He will call to the heavens above to
bring the soul,' 'and to the earth' to bring the body, and
thereafter, 'to judge His people.' '' (*Midrash Tannaim*
185).

4. Let the field and forest sing for joy; God comes to

judge the earth. God will judge the world with equity, and the nations with constancy (Psalm 96:13).

5. The Rabbis envisage God as sitting upon the throne of justice, and only after God is through viewing the world through the eyes of justice does God take His seat upon the throne of love and mercy. (Talmud *Rosh Hashanah* 17b).

6. The person who does not don the garment of the Torah and the *mitzvot* arrives at the heavenly tribunal in a state of nakedness (*Zohar* IV:174a).

7. When a soul is judged, it is asked: "Have you dealt justly?" (Talmud *Shabbat* 31).

8. Charity and lovingkindness are a powerful defense on the Day of Judgment (*Tosefta, Pe'ah* 1).

9. When God judges the world, He judges it according to the merits of the majority of the population (*Zohar* II:194a).

10. When God judges the earth, He judges first those who are influential (*Zohar Chadash* to Ruth, 76b).

11. Each night the soul of the one who sleeps goes before the Heavenly Tribunal. If it is found worthy, it is returned to the body (*Zohar* I:121a).

12. Rabbi Eliezer ben Jose Ha Gelili said: God's inclination in judgment is always found in man's favor. If nine hundred and ninety nine angels give a bad account of man, and only one a favorable account, God inclines the balance to the meritorious side. And even if nine hundred and ninety nine parts of the one angel's report are bad, and only one thousandth good, God will still do the same. (Jerusalem Talmud, *Kiddushin* 61d).

13. Unto God who orders judgment, and who searches hearts on the Day of Judgment (Rosh Hashanah morning liturgy).

14. Blessed are you, God, who is the True Judge (prayer recited by mourner when learning of the death of a loved one).

GOD'S LOVE FOR THE PEOPLE OF ISRAEL

The theme of God's special love for the people Israel reciprocated by Israel's love for God and the Torah is one which originated back in biblical times. God proclaims the children of Israel to be His special and treasured nation, and the Israelites promise to perform God's commandments. The Book the Song of Songs, traditionally read on Passover, is an allegorical love poem describing the relationship of God to the Jewish people. The liturgy, too, continues this expression of love for God in prayers such as *Ahavat Olam,* which proclaim God's eternal love for Israel. The Sephardic Jews have developed a beautiful ritual for the festival of Shavuot, when Jewish people everywhere commemorate the revelation of God atop Mount Sinai. Immediately after opening the ark on Shavuot morning, Sephardic Jews read a *ketubah,* a marriage contract between God (the groom) and Israel (the bride). In the *ketubah,* God invites the bride to the palace and promises to bind to her forever. The bride says, ''We will do and we will listen,'' the exact words that were used by the Israelites at Mount Sinai.

The following passages express God's love for Israel in a variety of ways.

1. Though it is written that God loves justice, the love God bears for His son Israel prevails over His love for justice (*Zohar* III:99b).

2. If the children of Israel but knew how much God loves them, they would run to Him with the strength of a lion (*Zohar* II:5b).

3. "My beloved is like a gazelle or a young hart" (Song of Songs 2:9). As a gazelle leaps and skips from bush to bush, from covert to covert, from hedge to hedge, so likewise does the Holy One, blessed be He, pass from synagogue to synagogue, and from academy to academy, that He may bless Israel (*Yalkut Shimoni* 1070).

4. Hillel said in the name of God by way of illustration of the covenant of love between God and Israel: "My feet carry me to the place which My heart loves. If thou comest to My house I will come to thine; but if thou comest not to My house I will not come to thine" (*Tosefta, Sukkah* 4:3).

5. Rabbi Akiba stressed the image of God in humanity when he said: "Beloved is man, for he is created in God's image, and it was a special token of love that he became conscious of it. Beloved is Israel, for they are called the children of God, and it was a special token of love that they became conscious of it" (*Ethics of the Fathers* 3:18).

6. Come and see how beloved of God are the children of Israel, for wherever they were exiled God went into exile with them (Talmud *Megillah* 29).

7. Deep is your love for us, Lord our God, boundless Your tender compassion (*Ahavah Rabbah* prayer in the daily liturgy).

8. With everlasting love have you loved your people Israel, teaching us Torah and *mitzvot*, statutes and laws. . . . Never take away Your love from us. Praised are You, God, who loves His people Israel (*Ahavat Olam* prayer, Friday-evening liturgy).

9. Thus says God: I will betroth you to Me forever. I will betroth you with righteousness, with justice, with love, and with compassion. I will betroth you to Me with faithfulness, and you shall love God (Hosea 2:21 –22).

10. Israel is more beloved by the Holy One than the ministering angels . . . for the ministering angels do not utter song above until Israel first utters it below (Talmud *Chullin* 91b).

11. Beloved are Israel, for when God calls them by a pet name, He calls them "priests," as it is said, "You shall be called the priests of the Lord" (Isaiah 61:6) (*Sifre,* Numbers 119).

FEAR OF GOD

The fear of God may indeed be the beginning of wisdom and the cornerstone of proper living, as the Bible repeatedly states. But "the fear of God" does not mean being afraid of God. The fear of God is not fear as we generally use the word today, but awe and reverence and respect.

Here are some passages that describe the fear of God in Jewish tradition.

1. We read: "Return o backsliding children" (Jeremiah 3:14). And we also read: "I will heal their backsliding" (Hosea 14:5). If Israel repents from love of

God, he needs no cure; if from fear, he must first be healed (Talmud *Yoma* 87).

2. Fear Heaven, for everything comes from Heaven (*Midrash ha-Gadol* 503).

3. A person is more feared by outsiders than by his intimates, but the fear of God is more recognized by those who are near to Him (*Mechilta Beshallach* 8).

4. Everything is in the hands of Heaven except the fear of heaven (Talmud *Berakhot* 33).

5. The person who possess the fear of God deserves to attain to the love of God (*Zohar* II:216a).

6. A robber, according to the Torah, must return the article he has stolen, but a thief must make double restitution. Why? It is because the robber demonstrates that he considers the fear of man equal in importance to the fear of God, but the thief fears man without fearing God (*Zohar* III:16a).

7. Fear is the primary element in the service a man should offer to his Master, namely, he must first show that he fears the Lord. Eventually the man will perform with joy the ordinances of the Lord (*Zohar* III:56a).

8. Great is fear in the presence of God, for fear includes humility, and humility includes piety. It will be found that the person who has the fear of Heaven has every virtue, but the person who is not God-fearing has neither humility nor piety (*Zohar* IV:145a).

9. The Psalmist assures us that the person who is God fearing will lack for nothing (Introduction to *Tikkune Zohar* 12a).

10. If there is no fear there is no wisdom nor learning, for fear is the storehouse of wisdom, and wisdom is a symbol of the valuables stored in reverence. Fear secretes

wisdom within itself. Fear is the palace of the King wherein valuables are housed (*Tikkune Zohar* 31b).

11. The person who observes the commandments to fear God observes all the commandments of the Torah, for fear is the gateway to them all (Introduction to *Tikkune Zohar* 11b).

12. There are three forms of fear: some fear God because they are afraid they will lose life and property; some fear God because they are afraid to lose their share in the World to Come. These two forms are imperfect. The perfect form is to fear God because He is the Master and the Ruler, and deserves obedience (Introduction to *Tikkune Zohar* 11b).

13. Unite our hearts to love and fear You. Then we will never be brought to shame (*Ahavah Rabbah* prayer, Sabbath morning liturgy).

14. "Many waters cannot quench love" (Canticles VIII:7). If the idolatrous nations of the world were to unite to destroy the love between God and Israel, they would be unable to do so (*Exodus Rabbah, Vayakhel* XLIX:1).

15. The Rabbis noticed that in Numbers 8:19 the words "the children of Israel" occurs five times. So they say: See how God loves the Israelites. In one single verse God names them five times! Rabbi Simeon ben Yochai said: Like a king who entrusted his son to a tutor, and kept asking, "Does my son eat, does he drink, has he gone to school, has he come back from school?" So God yearns to make mention of the Israelites at every hour (*Pesikta Kahana* 17a).

16. The Lord appeared of old unto me, saying, "I have loved you with an everlasting love" (Jeremiah

31:3). It does not say, "with abounding love" but "with everlasting love." For you might think the love with which God loves Israel was for three years or two years or a hundred years. But it was a love for everlasting and to all eternity (*Tanchuma de b. Elihahu,* p. 31.).

17. God said to Israel, "You have made me the only object of your love in the world, so I shall make you the only object of my love in the world" (*Talmud Berakhot* 6a).

LOVE OF GOD

"You shall love the Lord your God with all your heart, and all your soul and all of your might" (Deuteronomy 6:5). This verse affirms that the love for God is one of the first principles of Judaism. If it is true that many religions originated in fear of the unknown, Judaism, at a very early stage in its development, saw the greater good in loving God.

The following passages relate to a person's love of God.

1. Love God even though God slays you; for are we not taught to love God with our very souls? And what does this mean but that we are to love God even if God takes the soul from us (*Sifre* to Deuteronomy 6:5).

2. Those who serve God from love will be like servants who lay out gardens and delights with which to please their absent Lord when he returns (*Tana d'be Eliyahu* 560).

3. "And you shall love God"—namely, you shall make God beloved (Talmud *Yoma* 86).

4. Lovers of God are of two kinds: some love God because God gave them wealth, power, and length of life. Had they lacked these they might have felt the reverse towards Him. Others love God because God is their beloved Master whether He gives them good or evil (Introduction to *Zohar* 12a).

5. Rabbi Akiva said: " 'You shall love God . . . with all your might' (Deuteronomy 6:5)—in whatever measure God metes out to you, whether it be the measure of good or the measure of punishment" (*Yalkut* I:837).

6. "You shall love the Lord your God, with all your heart, with all your soul, and with all your might" (Deuteronomy 6:5).

7. Rabbi Joshua ben Levi said: Not even an iron wall can separate Israel from their Father in Heaven (Talmud *Sotah* 38b).

THE GOD OF MERCY

One of God's attributes is His attribute of tender mercy and grace. The following passages relate to God's mercies.

1. The Lord of Mercy does not begin His punishment with the taking away of life (*Leviticus Rabbah* 17:5).

2. God judges the nations at night when they perform no evil. God judges the children of Israel during the day when they perform *mitzvot* (Talmud *Avodah Zarah* 3).

3. Even in His anger, God always remembers to send a share of His mercies (Talmud *Pesachim* 50).

4. It is written (Psalm 62:13): "Also unto You, O God, belongs mercy." And further it is written: "For

you render unto every person according to his work."
In the beginning God wished to render justice but
when He observed that the world could not rest on
justice alone, He rendered mercy (Talmud *Rosh Hashanah* 17).

5. It is thus that God prays: "May it please Me that My
mercy may overcome My anger; that all My attributes
may be invested with compassion and that I may deal
with My children in the attribute of kindness, and that
out of regard for them I may omit judgment" (Talmud
Berakhot 7a).

6. Twenty-six times does the refrain "His mercy en-
dures forever" occur in the 136th Psalm, to match the
twenty-six generations that lived before the Law was
given, but whom God nourished with His grace (Talmud *Pesachim* 118a).

7. God was heard praying: "Oh that My attribute of
mercy may prevail over my attribute of justice, so that
grace alone may be bestowed upon My children on
earth" (Talmud *Berakhot* 7a).

8. Once Rabbi Judah the Prince sat and taught the
Law before an assembly of Babylonian Jews in Sep-
phoris, and a calf passed before him. It came and sought
to conceal itself, and began to moo, as if to say, "Save
me." Then he said, "What can I do for you? For this lot
you were created." Hence Rabbi Judah suffered a toothache for thirteen years. . . . After that a reptile ran past
his daughter, and she wanted to kill it. He said to her,
"Let it be, for it is written, 'His mercies are over all His
works.' " So it was said in heaven, "Because he had
pity, pity shall be shown to him." And his toothache
ceased (*Genesis Rabbah,* Noah 33:3).

9. The Lord, the Lord God, merciful and gracious, long-suffering and abundant in goodness and truth. Keeping mercy unto the thousandth generation . . . (Exodus 34:6–7).

THE IMMANENCE
AND TRANSCENDENCE OF GOD

Different names that have been given to God over the centuries create feelings of association that relate to a person's feelings of distance or closeness to Him. Theology calls this phenomenon the transcendence and immanence of God. For example, when God is referred to as the Sovereign King, the relationship that a human can have with Him appears to lie beyond the limits of ordinary experience. This is the transcendentalism of God. On the other hand, when God is called our Shepherd or Father, people often feel more of a sense of closeness to these metaphoric images of God. This is the immanence of the God experience, with a God image with which people often feel more comfortable.

The idea of the immanence and transcendence of God appears in the Talmud (*Megillah* 31a). In this section of the Talmud, several verses are presented that portray these two aspects of God, juxtaposed one with the other:

"For the Lord your God, He is the God of gods and Lord of lords" (Deuteronomy 10:17), and immediately afterward, "He does execute justice for the fatherless and widow."

This idea is repeated in the Prophets: "For thus says the High and Lofty One, that inhabits eternity, whose name is holy" (Isaiah 57:15) and it says immediately afterward, "I dwell with him that is of a contrite and humble spirit."

It is stated a third time in the Writings, as it is written: "Extol him that rides upon the skies, whose name is the Lord," (Psalm 68:5) and immediately afterward it is written, "A father of the fatherless and a judge of the widows."

The following examples portray both the concepts of nearness to and distance from God.

1. Let God be your companion (*Midrash Tehillim* to Psalm 104:1).

2. Man could conceive His abode as the very heavens and yet feel so close to Him that when he prays to Him it is "like a man who talks into the ear of his friend" (Jerusalem Talmud *Berakhot* 9:13a).

3. The Lord is my shepherd, I shall not be lacking (Psalm 23:1).

4. God is near to all who call upon Him in truth (Psalm 145:18).

5. Penitents can come near to God in a single moment. Perfect righteous people, however, may be compelled to labor many years to come as near (*Zohar* I:129b).

6. The person who prides himself as a disciple of the Sages and is not really learned shall not be admitted into the enclosure of God (*Bava Batra* 98).

7. When a person smiles at his shadow it smiles back at him. By the same token God is your shadow. As you are to Him, so He is to you (Midrash quoted in *Shalach*).

8. Four classes of people will not be received into the Divine Presence: scoffers, liars, hypocrites, and those who retail slander. (*Sotah* 42a).

9. Seven attributes help to bring a person near to the Throne of Glory, and these are: wisdom, righteousness, judgment, grace, mercy, truth, and peace (*Avot de Rabbi Natan,* ch. 37).

10. Our Father our King, we have sinned before You (High Holy Day Liturgy).

11. You are far, farther than the heaven of heavens, and near, nearer than my body is to me (Bachya ben Asher, *Kad HaKemah*).

12. The idol is near, and is yet far. God is far, for is He not in the Heaven of Heavens? And yet, God is near. For a person enters a synagogue, and stands behind a pillar, and prays in a whisper and God hears his prayer, and so it is with all His creatures. Can there be a nearer God than this? He is as near to His creatures as the ear to the mouth (Jerusalem Talmud *Berakhot* 9:1).

GOD'S OMNISCIENCE AND OMNIPRESENCE

The notion of God's omniscience, of His being all-knowing, is a quality of God that is a fundamental principle of Jewish faith. This includes the belief that God's knowledge includes the past, present, and the future, and that it extends even to knowing the thoughts of people. Similarly, the notion of God's omnipresence—of His being present everywhere—is another quality of God that many people have come to embrace.

Here are some passages that relate to the omniscience and omnipresence of God.

1. You have searched me and known me, O God,
    You know when I sit down and when I stand up,

You discern my thought from afar,
You measure out my course and my camp,
And are intimately acquainted with all my ways.
For there is not a word on my tongue,
But, God, You know everything (Psalm 139:1ff).

2. We behold you as Judge and Witness, recording our secret thoughts and acts and setting the seal thereon (*Unetaneh Tokef* prayer, Rosh Hashanah liturgy).

3. Why is God called the *Makom?* (i.e., Place). Because He is the space of the entire universe (*Genesis Rabbah* 68:9).

4. A matron said to Rabbi Jose: "My god is greater than yours. When God revealed Himself to Moses, he did not flee, but when my god, the serpent, appeared there, Moses ran away."

The Rabbi replied: "Moses could escape from your god by retreating a few steps, but where could he have escaped from my God?" (*Exodus Rabbah* 3).

5. God appeared to Moses in a despised thorn bush, not in a carob tree or a fig tree, which people value, in order to teach that there is no place on earth void of the Divine Presence (*Exodus Rabbah* on verse 3:3).

6. No sin, however done in secrecy and in darkness, can escape the eye of God who fills Heaven and earth. Wherever we are, and in whatever state, God is present with us. (*Tanchuma Buber, Naso* 14b–15a)

7. A heretic once said sarcastically to Gamliel II: "You say that where ten persons assemble for worship, there the Divine majesty descends upon them. How many such majesties are there?"

To which Gamliel replied: "Does not the one orb of day send forth a million rays upon the earth? And should not the majesty of God, which is a million times brighter than the sun, be reflected in every spot on earth?" (*Sanhedrin* 39a).

8. On a certain boat were passengers of many different nationalities. A storm threatened to sink the vessel. Each man took into his hand his own particular religious image and offered prayer to it. But the storm only grew in fury.

They turned to a Jewish lad and begged him to pray to his God. As soon as he had completed his prayer, calm ensued.

When they arrived at the port, all the passengers, except the lad, were about to go on shore to make purchases. They inquired of the boy, and he said: "What do you wish of a despicable creature like myself?"

They answered: "Not you, but we are to be despised. Some of us have their gods in Babylonia; others in Persia; still others, with them on this boat. But none avails in danger. Yet your God is with you wherever you are, and He does what you petition Him to do" (Jerusalem Talmud *Berakhot* 9).

9. A heathen asked Rabbi Joshua ben Karcha: "Why did God reveal Himself to Moses in a bush?"

The Rabbi answered: "To teach us that God is everywhere, even in a wild, lowly bush" (*Exodus Rabbah* 2).

ISRAEL'S RELATIONSHIP TO GOD

One of the most dominating themes expressed in the Bible is that the Jewish people are God's chosen people.

The first mention of the election of Israel occurs when God chose the first patriarch of Israel. In Genesis 12:1–3, God says to Abraham: "Get out of your country . . . and go into the land that I will show you, and I will make of you a great nation and I will bless you, and make your name great and be a blessing."

The following passages portray various themes related to Israel's relationship to God.

1. At the time you conduct yourself like sons of God, you are called His sons (Talmud *Kiddushin* 36).

2. An Israelite who has sinned is still an Israelite (Talmud *Sanhedrin* 21).

3. God dealt with Israel even as a mother hen deals with her chicks. When they are tiny, she feeds and warms them. When they are grown, she tells them: "Go and dig in the earth." When Israel was young, God sent him manna, and illumined his path at night. When Israel was grown, God told Israel: "Go and dig in the ground for your food" (Leviticus 19:23) (*Leviticus Rabbah* 25).

4. Rabbi Judah ben Ilai said that only when the children of Israel behaved like sons were they called the sons of God.

Rabbi Meir said: "Whether they are righteous or sinful, they are called the sons of God. We find in the Scripture that they are called foolish sons, untrustworthy sons, vicious sons, but sons notwithstanding" (Talmud *Kiddushin* 36a).

5. A philosopher asked Rabban Gamliel: "Do you have authority for maintaining that God will redeem you?" Rabbi Gamliel answered: "Yes." "This is an unfounded assertion," rejoined the philosopher. "Does

not Hosea say: 'He has loosed himself from them?' (5:6) And can, then, a woman who was loosed by a man, marry the man?'' (Deuteronomy 25:9). Rabbi Gamliel answered: "Who does the loosening, the man or the woman?'' "The woman,'' was the response. "Then what does it avail if God loosed Himself from us? The congregation of Israel is like unto the wife, and God is like unto the husband. And if we have not loosed Him, His loosening is valueless'' (*Shocher Tov* 10).

6. "You have seen what I did to the Egyptians and how I bore you on eagles' wings, and brought you to Me. Now, therefore, if you will listen to Me and keep my covenant, then you shall be My own treasure from all peoples; for all the earth is Mine. And you shall be to Me a Kingdom of Priests and a Holy Nation'' (Exodus 19:4–6).

7. "God has chosen you to be God's treasure from all the peoples that are upon the face of the earth. God did not set His love upon you, nor choose you, because you were more in number than any other people—for you were the fewest of all peoples—but because God loved you'' (Deuteronomy 7:6–8).

8. Behold, unto God belongs the heavens and the heaven of heavens, the earth, with all that is therein. Only God had a delight in your ancestors to love them and God chose their seed after them, even you, above all peoples, as it is this day (Deuteronomy 10:14–15).

9. Praised are You, God, who has chosen Your people Israel for Your service (Prayer *Ahavah Rabbah,* daily liturgy).

10. It is our duty to praise God for all . . . God has not made us like the other nations of the world, nor has God

placed us like the families of the earth. God has not made our destiny as theirs . . . (*Aleynu* prayer, daily liturgy).

11. You alone, O Israel, have I singled out of all the families of the earth. That is why I call you to account for all of your sins (Amos 3:2).

12. But you, Israel, My servant Jacob, whom I have chosen. Seed of Abraham, My friend . . . I chose you, I have not rejected you. Fear not, for I am with you. Don't be frightened, for I am your God. I strengthen you and I help you. I uphold you with My victorious right hand (Isaiah 41:8–10).

13. I am God, I have called you in righteousness . . . I have given you a covenant to the people, for a light to the nations, to open the eyes that are blind (Isaiah 42:6–7).

14. Rabbi Joshua ben Levi said: Not even an iron wall can separate Israel from their Father in Heaven (Talmud *Sotah* 38b).

15. "I am sick of love" (Song of Songs 2,5). The congregation of Israel says to God, "Lord of the world, all the sickness which you bring upon me is only for the purpose of making me love you. . . . All the sicknesses, which the nations bring upon me are only because I love you" (*Song of Songs Rabbah* II:5).

16. It is noticed as two of the marks of the Israelite that he should "penetrate to the very essence of the Law and love God with a perfect love, whether good befalls him or evil" (*Leviticus Rabbah, Vayikra* 3:7).

SANCTIFICATION AND PROFANATION OF GOD'S NAME

The assertion that a person, with all his limitations and faults, can hallow God, and that God requires people to hallow his name, is known in rabbinic literature as *kiddush haShem*. Human beings may be sanctified by God if they choose to follow God's commandments. It is likewise the duty of man to hallow God. "I will be hallowed among the children of Israel; I am the Lord who hallows you," proclaims the Torah. This verse was originally directed to the priesthood, who, as guardians of the ancient sanctuary, were warned in this manner to fulfill their duties to God. Later, however, the obligation to sanctify God's name was extended to the "kingdom of priests"—the whole Jewish people. Any extraordinary act that would bring honor to the Jewish people was considered an example of sanctifying God's name. The most extreme form of sanctification of God's name is martyrdom, the willingness to forgo the privilege of living, if necessary, to prevent the desecration of God's name.

The opposite of the sanctification of God's name is *chillul hashem,* profanation of God's name. Profaning God's name was an act that caused a person to withdraw from God. Any immoral act that is committed is considered a profanation of God's holy name.

The following passages cite references to both the sanctification and profanation of God's name.

1. Rabbi Yochanan ben Berokah said: "If a person profanes the Name of God secretly, he will be requited openly. In the profanation of the Name, there is no distinction of inadvertent and presumptuous" (*Ethics of the Fathers* 4:5).

2. When experience showed that the pagan neighbors of the Jews never returned anything which they had found, belonging to a Jew, it was decided in law that

a Jew might keep the possession of an idolater which he had found. Some rabbis, however, decreed that it glorified God's Name to return things found in this way.

Simeon ben Shetach bought a donkey. Under its saddle he discovered a pearl, left there by mistake. He returned it to the Arab who then exclaimed: "Blessed be the God of Israel." The Rabbi's disciples inquired why he had not kept that which he had found, in accordance with the law. The Rabbi answered: "Am I then a barbarian? His blessing is worth more to me than all the money that the pearl might have brought" (Talmud *Bava Metziah* 2).

3. Rabbi Ishmael taught: While other classes of sins are atoned for, according to their heinousness, by repentance, the Day of Atonement, and chastisement cumulatively, not all together suffice to atone for the person through whom the Name of God is profaned. Such guilt is wiped out only by the day of death (Talmud *Yoma* 86a).

4. Better that a letter of the sacred Torah itself be blotted out than the Divine Name be profaned (Talmud *Yevamot* 79a).

5. When Elijah enjoined the priests of Baal to choose one bullock as a sacrifice to Baal while he chose one bullock as a sacrifice to God (1 Kings 18:23), the bullock chosen by the priests refused to accompany them. The animal cried aloud: "We are both twins and we grew up together. Why should my brother go to God and I to the Baal?"

Elijah answered the bullock: "Go with them, for you will sanctify God's Name as truly as your brother."

Nevertheless the bullock refused to go until Elijah led it to the altar of Baal (*Numbers Rabbah,* 23).

GOD'S UNITY

One of the fundamental principles of Jewish people related to God is that God is One and His Name is One. It is believed that God is not only One but unique in every way. No human being is comparable to God in capacity or degree of perfection.

The following passages deal with God's unity.

1. The Rabbis ask: "And is not God One? What do these words mean: 'In that day God shall be One and His name shall be One'?"

The answer: "Now God is One, but His names are many. Everyone conceives Him according to his own vision. But in the world that is to be—in that glorious future that is yet to come—not only will God be One, but His Name too, will then be One" (Talmud *Pesachim* 50a).

2. A Jew is the person who opposes every sort of polytheism (Talmud *Megillah* 13a).

3. A person should proclaim God's unity with his lips by reciting the *Shema.* He should feel it in his heart. He should think of it in his mind (*Zohar* I:242a).

4. Rabbi Nathan said: "Some theologians argue that a multiple nature of the Godhead may be learned from the phrase: 'Let us make man in our image' (Genesis 1:26). How can they then explain the phrase: 'I will blot out man whom I have created'?" (Genesis 6:7).

If two who build a house are partners, may only one destroy it? (Introduction to *Tanchuma Buber* 154).

5. Hear O Israel, the Lord is our God, the Lord is One (Deuteronomy 6:4).

6. Such is the assurance of Your prophet Zechariah: The Lord shall be acknowledged King of all the earth.

On that day the Lord shall be One and His name One
(*Aleynu* prayer, daily liturgy).

7. One is our God, great our Lord, holiness is His
nature (liturgy of Torah service).

8. There is a Creator who alone created and creates
all things. He is One and Unique (*Yigdal* prayer, Friday
evening liturgy).

9. Know this day, and lay it to your heart, that the
Lord He is God in heaven and upon the earth beneath;
there is none else (Deuteronomy 4:39).

10. See now that I, even I, am He,
And there is no God with Me.
I kill, and I make alive;
I have wounded and I heal;
And there is none that can deliver out of My
hand (Deuteronomy 32:39).

11. Hear O Israel, the Lord our God, the Lord is One.
It is as if the Holy One, blessed be He, said to Israel:
"Look, My sons, at all that I have created. Everything I
have created in pairs. The heavens and the earth, the
moon and the sun, the male and the female, this world
and the World to Come—all have been paired. But My
glory is alone, it is unique, in all the universe" (*Deuteronomy Rabbah* 2).

GOD RECEIVES THE PENITENT

The tenderness of God, the desire to bring back, save,
and forgive His people is strikingly shown in many

passages about repentance. Here are some passages that relate to God opening His heart to those who repent.

1. As soiled garments can be cleansed, so the Israelites, albeit they sin, can return by repentance to God (*Exodus Rabbah, Beshallach* 23:10).

2. Rabbi Chelbo said To Rabbi Samuel ben Nachmani: "Since I have heard that you are a good Haggadist, tell me the meaning of Lamentations 3:44, 'You have covered yourself with a cloud that our prayers should not pass through.' " He replied, "Prayer is likened to a bath, repentance to the sea. As the bath is sometimes open and sometimes shut, so the gates of prayer are sometimes shut and sometimes open, but as the sea is always open, so the gates of repentance are always open. When a man wishes to bathe in the sea, he can bathe in it at any hour he likes. So with repentance, whenever a man wishes to repent, God will receive him." But Rabbi Anan said: "The gates of prayer, too, are never shut" (*Lamentations Rabbah* 3:60).

3. If a person were to come and say that God does not receive the penitent, Manasseh would come and testify against him, for there was never a man more wicked than he, and yet, in the hour of his repentance, God received him, as it is said, "He prayed to God, and God was entreated of him" (2 Chronicles 33:13) (*Numbers Rabbah, Naso* 14:1).

4. "Open to me, my sister." Rabbi Issi said: God says to the Israelites, open to me, my children, the gate of repentance as minutely as the point of a needle, and I will open for you gates wide enough for carriages and wagons to enter through them. Rabbi Levi said: If the Israelites would but repent for one day, they would be

redeemed, and the son of David would come straight away, as it says, "Today, if you would hear his voice" (Psalm 45:7) (*Song of Songs Rabbah* 5:2).

5. God says to the Israelites, "Repent before I return to the attribute of judgment, for then I should not know how to act; repent while I stand upon the attribute of mercy, and then I can receive you" (*Pesikta Rabbati* 182b).

6. Rabbi Judah Nesiah said in the name of Rabbi Judah ben Simeon: If a person shoots an arrow, it may reach one field's length or two, but greater is the power of repentance, for it reaches to the throne of glory (*Pesikta Kahana* 163b).

7. If your sins are as high as heaven, even unto the seventh heaven, and even to the throne of glory, and you repent, I will receive you (*Pesikta Rabbati* 185a).

8. To an earthly king, a person goes full, and returns empty; to God, he goes empty, and returns full (*Pesikta Rabbati* 185a).

9. A king had a son who had gone astray from his father a journey of a hundred days. His friends said to him, "Return to your father"; he said, "I cannot." Then his father sent to say, "Return as far as *you* can, and *I* will return to you" (*Pesikta Rabbati* 184b).

10. Rabbi Elazar said: If a person treats his fellow with contempt in public, and afterwards seeks to be reconciled with him, the other says, "You treated me contemptuously in public, and now you want to be reconciled with me between ourselves. Go and bring the men before whom you treated me contemptuously. Then will I be reconciled with you." But God does not act thus. A man stands and reviles and blasphemes Him

in the open street, and God says, "Repent between ourselves, and I will receive you" (*Pesikta Kahana* 163b).

GOD THE UNKNOWABLE

These verses convey the theological notion that God is so beyond all others that to man God is a mystery.

1. Oh God, what mysteries I find in You;
   How vast are the number of Your purposes,
   I try to count them, they are more than the sand,
   I wake from my reverie, and I am still lost in You
   (Psalm 139:17,18).

2. Give ear to this, O Job,
   Stand still and consider the wonders of God.
   Do you know when God does His work
   And causes the light of His cloud to shine?
   Do you know regarding the balancing of a cloud,
   The wonders of the one perfect in knowledge?
   (Job 37:14).

3. If I knew Him I would be Him *(Saadia Gaon).*

4. Where were you when I laid the foundations of the earth?
   Declare, if you have the insight . . .
   Have you ever in your life commanded the morning?
   Or assigned its place to the dawn? . . .

Have you gone to the sources of the sea,
Or walked in the hollows of the deep?
Have the gates of death been revealed to you?
 . . . (Job 38:1–6).

NAMES OF GOD

It is curious that Jewish tradition, which places such a strong emphasis on the One God concept, possesses such a large number of names for the Divine. In the plethora of names, appellations, and descriptions of God found in Jewish tradition, each connotes a quality or aspect of God. Here is a partial list of God's names as they appear throughout Jewish literature and liturgy.

1. *Adonai,* My Lord
2. Lord
3. The Divinity
4. Mighty One of Jacob
5. Most High
6. Almighty God
7. God of the Covenant
8. Everlasting Rock
9. Everlasting Arms
10. Lord of Hosts
11. Holy One
12. Shepherd of Israel
13. King of Israel
14. Former of All
15. Guardian of Israel
16. Rock of Israel
17. King
18. The true God
19. *El*
20. Everlasting God
21. God of Vision
22. Ancient God
23. I am that I am
24. God of Truth
25. Praiseworthy God
26. Shield of Abraham
27. King of Kings
28. The Name
29. Heaven
30. Awesome One
31. Eternal One
32. Lover of Israel

33. Redeemer
34. God of our ancestors
35. Mighty One
36. Rescuer
37. Father of mercy
38. The Place
39. Faithful One
40. Infinite One
41. Rock of Ages
42. Master of All
43. Our Shepherd
44. Our Healer
45. Compassionate One
46. Bountiful One
47. Peace
48. Judge of the Earth
49. Ransomer
50. Living God
51. Reviver of the Dead
52. Lord of the Universe
53. Our Father in Heaven
54. The Good One
55. Holy King
56. Patient One
57. Hidden of Hiddens
58. The Eternal
59. First Cause
60. Lord, Man of War

Here is a cross-section of verses in which various names of God appear.

1. The Lord is my Shepherd, I shall not want (Psalm 23:1).

2. Rock of Ages, let our song praise Your saving power (*Ma'oz Tzur,* a popular Hanukkah hymn).

3. Our Father, Our King, we have sinned before You (Prayer *Avinu Malkenu,* found in the High Holy Day liturgy).

4. The Lord eternal reigned before the birth of every living thing (Prayer *Adon Olam,* found in daily liturgy).

5. Moses said to God, "When I come to the Israelites and say to them 'The God of your fathers has sent me to you,' and they ask me, 'What is His name?' what shall I

say to them?'' And God said to Moses, ''I am that I am'' (Exodus 3:13–14).

6. We wish you peace, attending angels, angels of the most sublime, the King of Kings, the Holy One, Praised be He (Prayer *Shalom Aleichem* in Friday-evening liturgy).

7. God is the space of the world? What is the world? The Shechinah (*Zohar* 4:242a).

8. Rabbi Ammi said: ''Why is God given the name of 'place'?'' Because He is the place (Hebrew *makom*) of the world, and the world is not His place. Rabbi Abba ben Yudan said: The matter is like a warrior who rides upon a horse, and his weapons hang down on each side. The horse is an adjunct and secondary to the rider, but the rider is not an adjunct and secondary to the horse (*Genesis Rabbah, Vayetze* 68:9).

9. The Lord is a ''Man of War . . .'' (Exodus 15:3).

10. And God spoke to Moses, and said to him: ''I am the Lord, and I appeared unto Abraham, Isaac, and Jacob as 'El Shaddai' (i.e., God Almighty), but by My name 'Adonai' I made Me not known to them'' (Exodus 6:2).

11. In the beginning *Elohim* created the heaven and the earth (Genesis 1:1).

12. Holy, holy is the Lord of Hosts, the whole world is filled with His glory (Isaiah 6:3).

13. Praised are You, God, Shield of Abraham *(Amidah)*.

14. Guardian of the people Israel, guard the remnant of Israel and let not Israel perish, those who say Shema Yisrael (Prayer *Shomer Yisrael*).

15. Father of mercy, show us mercy (Prayer *Ahavah Rabbah*).

16. I am grateful to you, living, enduring King, for restoring my soul to me in compassion. You are faithful beyond measure (Prayer *Modeh Ani,* traditionally recited upon rising in the morning).

17. God of retribution, Lord, God of retribution appear. Judge of the earth, give the arrogant their deserts (Psalm 94:1).

18. Dwelling in the shelter of the Most High, abiding in the shadow of the Almighty, I call the Lord my refuge and fortress, my God in whom I trust (Psalm 91:1).

19. Praised are You, God, Master of Life and death (*Amidah* prayer).

20. Praised are You, God, Redeemer of the people Israel (*Amidah* prayer).

21. Praised are You, God, beneficent God, to whom all praise is due (*Amidah* prayer).

GLOSSARY

Adonai: Personal name of the God of Israel, written in the Bible with the four consonants YHVH referred to as the tetragrammaton.

Agnosticism: Refers to a neutralist view on the question of the existence of God.

Animism: Belief that regards all objects and beings as possessed by spirits.

Anthropomorphism: Ascription of human form and characteristics to God.

Atheism: The disbelief in the existence of deity.

Cosmogony: Theory of the origin of the universe.

Cosmology: Metaphysics that deals with the universe as an orderly system.

Covenant Theology: Theological system based on the fundamental relationship in which the individual Jew stands, namely, the covenant. This covenant was made and maintained in the context of the community where the individual Jew's relationship with God was established. Thus, the individual's and the people's relationship to God is of primary importance to Judaism and the Jewish people.

Creatio ex nihilo: Creation from nothing; the theological notion that God created the world out of nothing.

Da'at Elohim: Knowledge of God.

"Death of God": Philosophical and theological post-Holocaust concept that God "died" because God did not stop the events of the Holocaust.

Deism: Movement of thought advocating natural religion based on human reason rather than revelation, emphasizing morality. In the eighteenth century, it denied the interference of the Creator with the laws of the universe.

Devekut: Literally, the cleaving of a person to God. A mystical concept.

Din Ve'cheshbon: A judgment and accounting of the individual by God.

Divine Attributes: Characteristics or behaviors of God.

Dualism: Doctrine that the universe is under the dominion of two opposing principles, one of which is good and the other evil.

Dynamism: Primitive religious belief that the supernatural is a general indefinable form of mysterious power found in almost everything.

Eclipse of God: Like the Hebrew *hester panim,* this is when God hides His face, often as a form of retribution.

Ein Sof: The Infinite One, the name for God in the kabbalistic mystical movement.

Elohim: One of God's biblical names, *Elohim* (plural of *El*).

El Shaddai: Divine name frequently found in the Bible, often translated "Almighty."

Epikoros: Also spelled *apikorus,* a rabbinic term for a nonbeliever in God or a skeptic.

Ethical Monotheism: The notion that this is the essential element of Judaism once all ritual and ceremony is stripped away. The belief in one God who is the standard for ethics in the world.

Everything is foreseen, yet permission is given: The classic statement of Rabbi Akiba in *Ethics of the Fathers,* which expresses the reconciliation between God's omniscience and the notion of free will. The individual is free to do what is chosen, but God knows ahead of time what the choice will be.

Everything is in the Hands of Heaven: The classic statement that expresses utter abandon to God, who is in control of everything in the universe.

Existentialism: Movement in philosophy that stresses that people are entirely free and therefore responsible for what they make of themselves.

Free Will, Doctrine of: Philosophical notion that allows for the individual to select a course of action from a number of choices and is the cause of the action that results from his choice.

Gnosticism: Reflecting a schism in the world between light (good) and darkness (evil), it is a mystical system, based on *gnosis* (knowledge of God).

HaMakom: Literally "the place," a name for God.

Henotheism: Refers to the belief in one God, yet not excluding all other gods. Henotheists depict God as a personified national spirit, a national God, rather than as an international or universal God.

"Hester Panim": Referring to God when He hides His face as a sign of retribution.

Holy One (Blessed be He), The: The commonly used name for God, especially in rabbinic literature.

Humanism: Antithetical to supernaturalism, humanism regards God as man's highest aspirations, reflecting man's pursuit of ideal values and embodying the sum of humanity.

I am that I Am: The answer that Moses received from God when he asked God for the Divine Name in the area of the burning bush (Exodus 3:13–14). Often understood as "God will be as God will be."

I and Thou: Phrase associated with Martin Buber that epitomizes his belief that all experience is based on relationships. Everyday experiences are "I-It," but true communication between people is on a higher plane, reflected by a relationship between the individual and God, the Eternal Thou.

Kavod: Referring to God, this term reflects God's presence.

"Kelippot": According to the Kabbalah, these "shells" or "husks" are forces of evil that dominate the spiritual lights originally emanating from creation.

Kingdom of God: A reference to God's sovereignty in which God will be acknowledged as the only God, when all humans will accept God's rule. In Hebrew, it translates *malchut shaddai.*

Lord of Hosts. In Hebrew, *Adonai Tzevaot,* one of God's many names.

Lord of the World: Generally used to express the belief that the person God of Israel, *Adonai,* is also the universal God of the world.

Monotheism: Belief in one God, supreme over all.

Naturalism: Belief that the world can be explained in terms of scientifically verifiable ideas.

Negative Attributes, Doctrine of: As articulated by Maimonides, once one begins to try to list the attributes of God, knowing full well that the list must be concluded without fully expressing all the attributes, we therefore limit God. As a result, we should not try to list any attributes.

Numinous: Filled with a sense of the presence of the divinity.

Ontological Argument: Attempt to prove the existence of God from the idea or definition of God.

Paganism: Belief in false gods.

Pantheism: Philosophy that equates God with the forces and laws of the universe.

Particularism: A focus on Israel's unique relationship with God rather than God's general relationship with the world.

Polytheism: Belief in many gods.

"Radical Amazement": Phrase coined by Abraham Joshua Heschel, it refers to individual experiences of the Divine in this world, arguing for an extraordinary sensitivity to the hidden reality inherent in the seemingly ordinary.

Rationalism: Reliance on reason as the basis for establishment of religious truth.

Redemption: Generally refers to deliverance by God. In philosophy a sign that God has triumphed over evil.

Religious Empiricism: Knowledge of the existence and nature of God as originating through a person's sense experience.

Revelation: The act of communication from God to humans and the content of such a communication.

Reward and Punishment: A concept from rabbinic Judaism that suggests that God rewards good acts and punishes those who do evil.

Ruach Elohim: Literally, "the spirit of God" (as quoted in the creation story in the first chapter of Genesis). It may also be translated in philosophic terms as the essence of God.

Shechinah: A mystical concept, the indwelling presence of God on earth, also considered to be a feminine aspect of God.

Spirituality: A buzz word of the 1980s, it is an undefined term in Judaism (borrowed from Christianity) that reflects some sort of a sense of relationship of the individual with the Divine.

Teleology: The study of the evidences of the design of nature.

Theism: Belief in the existence of one God viewed as the creative source of man and the world who transcends yet is immanent in the world.

Theodicy: Defense of God's goodness and omnipotence in view of the existence of evil.

Theogony: An account of the origin and descent of the gods.

Theology: Literally "the study of God."

Theonomy: The state of being governed by God.

Theophany: Referring to any visible manifestation of a deity. One of the greatest theophanies in the Bible was the appearance of God to Moses on Mount Sinai.

Thirteen Attributes of God: Referring to the actions emanating from God, spoken of in the Torah (Exodus 34:6–7).

Tikkun: Literally "repair." According to the Kabbalah, it is essential to bring about world order by repairing the vessels that were broken by God at creation.

Totemism: A kind of early religion in which people felt themselves mystically bound with the spirit of a specific animal, plant, force of nature.

Transcendence and Immanence of God: Philosophical concept that describes the paradoxical concept of a Supreme Being who can be both "close" to humankind as well as "distant" from humankind.

Trinity: In Christianity, God the Father, the Son (Jesus), and the Holy Spirit, in which all are one, the same, and equal.

Tzimtzum: Literally, "constriction." In mysticism, it refers to God's self-concentration. In order to create the world, God constricts Himself.

When Bad Things Happen to Good People: A best-selling book by Rabbi Harold Kushner, an American Conservative rabbi that basically describes a limited God who does not directly impact on what happens to people in the world.

Yahweh: Believed to be the name of God among the Israelites starting with the time of Moses.

Yoke of the Kingdom: Acknowledge God as sovereign in the world. It reflects one's acceptance of God's commandments.

For Further Reading

This compilation could easily be expanded. It consists of books that I have found particularly useful in my research.

Agus, Jacob B. *Guideposts in Modern Judaism.* New York: Block Publishers, 1954.

Baeck, Leo. *The Essence of Judaism.* New York: Schocken, 1948.

Berkovits, Eliezer. *Man and God: Studies in Biblical Theology.* Detroit: Wayne State University Press, 1969.

Buber, Martin. *I and Thou.* New York: Scribner, 1958.

Gillman, Neil. *Sacred Fragments.* Philadelphia: Jewish Publication Society, 1990.

Glatzer, Nahum. *Franz Rosenzweig: His Life and Thought.* New York: Schocken, 1973.

Herberg, Will. *Judaism and Modern Man.* Philadelphia: Jewish Publication Society, 1951.

Heschel, Abraham J. *Between God and Man.* New York: The Free Press, 1959.

_____. *Man's Quest for God.* New York: Scribner, 1954.

Kaplan, Aryeh. *Maimonides' Principles: The Fundamentals of Jewish Faith*. New York: National Conference of Synagogue Youth, 1984.

Kaplan, Mordecai. *Judaism without Supernaturalism*. New York: Jewish Reconstructionist Press, 1958.

Kushner, Harold S. *When Children Ask about God*. New York: Schocken, 1976.

Neusner, Jacob, ed. *Understanding Jewish Theology*. New York: Ktav Publishers, 1973.

Siegel, Seymour, and Gertel, Elliot, eds. *God in the Teachings of Conservative Judaism*. New York: The Rabbinical Assembly, 1985.

Steinberg, Milton. *Basic Judaism*. New York: Harcourt, Brace and World, Inc., 1947.

Wolpe, David J. *The Healer of Shattered Hearts: A Jewish View of God*. New York: Henry Holt and Company, 1990.

Index

About the Author

Rabbi Ronald Isaacs is the spiritual leader of Temple Sholom in Bridgewater, New Jersey. He received his doctorate in instructional technology from Columbia University's Teacher's College. He is the author of numerous books, including *Loving Companions: Our Jewish Wedding Album*, coauthored with Leora Isaacs; *The Jewish Information Source Book: A Dictionary and Almanac*; Mitzvot: *A Sourcebook for the 613 Commandments; The Jewish Book of Numbers;* and *Words for the Soul: Jewish Wisdom for Life's Journey*. Rabbi Isaacs is currently on the editorial board of *Shofar* magazine and serves as vice president of the New Jersey Rabbinical Assembly. He resides in New Jersey with his wife, Leora, and their children, Keren and Zachary.